ELIZA

Gwyneth Millard

CHAPTER 1

Eliza was sitting on the edge of the little bridge over the river with her feet hovering as close to the water as possible without actually touching it. The skirt of her dress was spread out around her and leaning backwards upon her hands, she smiled serenely. The picture which presented itself on that bright sunny morning in 1872 might have seemed to have been carefully posed and to anyone who knew Eliza that would have seemed a reasonable assumption. Certainly she had seen her father arranging groups in his photography studio many times.

Eliza was deep in thought and looking straight ahead of her to where the river disappeared around the bend. She knew that if she followed the river along its course, she would eventually find herself in the Plantations, those beautiful but forbidden gardens which held such fascination for her.

She saw the tree-lined path which ran alongside the little river and in the distance she could see children playing on the grassy hillock to the right of the river. They were about the same age as her and yet she felt she had little in common with them. She had always felt like a spectator in most of the things she tried to do with other nine-year-old children. She watched them and wished she could be like them, but no matter how hard she tried she could not engage in their fun and games.

Eliza lived in a house which was full of children. James was seven, Alfred five, William three and Margaret, the baby of the family, was just one year old. Eliza had always had to be 'grown-up' and help to look after the younger ones. Perhaps this was why she found it so hard to behave like a child herself. Her father, James Millard, did not encourage friendships anyway. He considered that a large family was self-sufficient without any need for outsiders.

She was so busy with her own thoughts that she never heard Mac approaching. She had known he would appear eventually and that was probably why the scene had been so carefully arranged. Nine years old she might be in years but in the wiles and wisdom of women she was a match for those twice her age.

"Thinking Holy thoughts again Eliza, eh?" he teased.
Eliza looked round with a start. She was so happy to see Mac, her best friend. He was seventeen, almost a man really but they had always enjoyed being together ever since that day so many years ago when his father, a respected doctor in the town, had stopped to speak with Eliza's father while they were out walking.

'Mac' was Eliza's shortened version of his name. His full name was Edward Percy Plantaganet Macloghlin and Eliza had found that rather a mouthful when she first heard it. When his parents heard that she called him 'Mac' they disapproved; but then they disapproved of most of the things she did.

Eliza's father was a man for whom the doctor had great respect. Indeed Mac had once heard his father saying to his wife "that Millard fellow is the only person round here that has anything like sense to talk about. Some of his ideas are incredible; if only he had the money to put some of them into practice". Mac knew that 'sense' was very important to his father and he hoped that one day he himself might be able to prove that he had some of his own.

"Oh, you shouldn't creep up on me like that" Eliza said, "I might have fallen into the river"

"Well, I could have rescued you if you had done"

"I might have been already drowned and then you would have had to take my body home and tell my father that you had killed me"

2

Mac stood looking down at the beautiful little girl and he smiled.

"I would never let anything happen to you, Eliza," he said," I would bring you back to life with a special kiss".

One of the things Mac had always enjoyed doing had been walking. He was not a boy who liked the rough and tumble indulged in by other boys of his age. He was given to strong emotions and even his own parents found him quite difficult to understand. He longed for his mother to hold and comfort him but his father would not tolerate such behaviour and he had to be content with his own company for most of the time. As he was growing up he became more and more unhappy and chose a solitary existence for himself.

On one occasion he had been to the Lake District with his family but he had chosen to spend much of the time by himself. There he discovered his talent for writing poetry and from the age of eleven he wrote much beautiful verse.

He had few friends, since his school fellows chose to leave him alone rather than try to understand his ways. They sometimes wondered why he chose to talk to the little four year old girl at the other end of the long road. Mac himself wondered why a child as young as Eliza seemed to be able to offer him the contentment he never found with his family or with boys of his own age.

"I was wondering, Mac, was Jesus like you, always good and kind and wanting to help people?" Eliza looked up, questioning him.

Mac suddenly became very serious. He had hoped not to have to discuss his religious beliefs with Eliza. She was still very young and he thought she ought to have the opportunity to develop her own theories and not take hold of his indiscriminately.

"I think Jesus must have been a very clever man, Eliza, but I am not sure that he was what people said he was"

"You mean he wasn't the son of God?" Eliza was quite shocked by this statement from her young hero. This was not what she had been told at Sunday School.

"Look, Eliza, you shouldn't worry about that now. When you have learned a little more about the world you will be able to work things out for yourself without taking my word for it."

But Eliza had learned enough from Mac already to be able to judge that he was wise and good. If Mac had doubts about Jesus then she must think very carefully about what people told her in the future.

The two of them sat there for some time without speaking. To the onlooker it must have seemed a strange partnership. However they shared many of the same emotions and understood each other in a most uncanny way.

It was during one of the afternoons when he was with Eliza in the square, showing her the leaves beginning to appear on the trees and answering her endless questions that Mac began to realise what he wanted to do with his life. If he could bring such happiness and peace to a little child in this way and if it gave him such a feeling of satisfaction and achievement to do so, then why could he not do this as a doctor? His parents had high ideals and expectations for their two sons. As a highly qualified and experienced surgeon himself, his father hoped that they would follow him into the medical profession, but John had already made it plain that he wanted to become an engineer of some kind and Edward seemed to have his head so full of poetry that it was doubtful if he would ever do anything so scientific or practical.

It gave him immense delight therefore to hear his son say that he had decided he would like to take the preliminary medical examinations after all.

Mac was only thirteen when he entered and passed the tests set for him. Those marking the papers and interviewing him marvelled at his knowledge and depth of thought. His father was amazed but Mac knew that those same emotions which inspired him to write poetry were the very ones necessary to care for other human beings and to alleviate suffering.

At the age of fourteen, having passed the necessary examinations, Mac was taken on as an apprentice, articled to a local doctor. Three years later he became assistant to another doctor and this time proved so indispensable that it seemed to Mac and to others that he was in fact doing most of the work.

Eliza went to church on Sundays and listened to the stories of the miracle cures wrought by Jesus and wondered whether Mac actually was God. He could make people better and everyone who met him loved him at once.

His father was a little more satisfied with him now that he was being seen as a respectable doctor but still Mac could not feel loved by his own mother and father. He gave love to those who needed him and they gave him a kind of love in return but the two people whose love he really needed appeared to give him none.

Now that Mac was a doctor, the times when Eliza could talk to him were few and far between. She treasured their moments together. She shared with him the feeling of being unable to relate to her mother and father. They were both too busy with family matters and her father's inventions and photography to pay much attention to a very lonely and unhappy little girl.

Since Mac had been working for Doctor Jackson he had become increasingly puzzled by the attitude of the so-called Christians among his patients. It seemed strange to him that those who loved God and strove to get to Heaven became sick and anxious at the thought of actually going there. They had great faith that 'the young doctor' would keep them out of Heaven for the time being. In his opinion the most successful medicine was 'one tablespoonful of mixture and two tablespoonfuls of fun'.

Mac was a handsome, athletic young man, as physically fit as he was mentally clean. Many years later Eliza would write that 'He had a great love for both human beings and animals and each in his turn would come to understand his love and care and have reason to be grateful for it'

He was working hard to earn enough money to take him to University and to the hospital where he could train to become a fully qualified doctor. Eliza found she needed his help more than ever now and yet she did not want to worry him with her problems when his own were so much greater.

Eliza was being prepared for her Confirmation. The Vicar talked to the young people about the seriousness of this step, about what it would mean to their lives and how it was a natural progression from the christening that had taken place when they were babies and too young to understand the promises being made for them. This was a great worry to Eliza. First of all she wondered how her Godparents could have made promises for her when they did not know whether she would want to keep them or not. After all, they had no idea at the time of her Christening what kind of person she might grow up into. Then she wondered why they had never made any attempt to talk to her about her worries and doubts while they were supposedly keeping her on the straight and narrow path.

Despite these concerns, she felt she owed it to these people to go through with this Confirmation, since they had made the promises in good faith and were not to be blamed for her own doubts.

It was with much heart-searching, therefore, that Eliza set out for Church on the day of her Confirmation. She was wearing an all-white muslin dress, in common with all the other little girls. The boys wore new brown suits. On each girl's head was placed a small white veil and when Eliza's was in place she felt for a moment like a bride. She thought of the day she hoped one day might come, when she and Mac would be married. She imagined herself standing at the altar, just as she did now, wearing a white dress and with a veil over her face. She imagined how she would feel as Mac gently lifted up the veil and saw her beautiful face gazing up at him. Had her parents and Godparents been able to read her mind, they would have considered these thoughts totally inappropriate for an eleven-year-old girl during her Confirmation.

After the ceremony she was no less confused. She had learned her catechism well and had been accepted into the church and yet still there were doubts in her mind. Mac never tried to convince his little flower that the lessons she learned at Church were anything but true and yet she knew that those ideas were alien to his own.

Returning home from the service she met Mac standing by her house.

"Now, how does it feel to be a confirmed Christian?" he asked.
Eliza sensed a hint of sarcasm in his voice and in his smile and she wondered why he would never talk to her about Church.

They walked together down the hill and turned left towards the river where Eliza spent so many hours. Then they stepped down to the water's edge and began to walk along the little path. Soon the river wound round between the hills known locally as 'Bloody mountains' because a famous battle had been fought there during the Civil War. The children were playing there as usual but now Eliza looked at them

7

with new eyes. She would rather be with Mac than all the children in the world.

Mac taught her about the flowers and the birds and the animals. He taught her about people. He spoke to her about his hopes and ambitions and he helped her with the problems she found it difficult to discuss with anyone else.

Suddenly she realised that they were inside the Plantations, the grounds around the stately Haigh Hall where, so Aunt Lucy, her father's sister insisted, their ancestors, the Bradshaigh family, had lived. James and Lucy Millard's mother had been born Jane Bentley but it was thought that she was really a member of the family who lived at Haigh Hall. Since the Hall's residents were now the Lindsay family, the Bradshaigh name having died out in the absence of a male heir, no one could be quite certain that Jane was indeed part of that heritage. Aunt Lucy however, clung fiercely to the certainty that she was of noble birth.

There were so many trees. Huge rhododendrons crowded the sides of the paths; small animals darted for cover as they approached. Eliza began to think she had died and gone to Heaven. She said as much to Mac.

"This is Heaven, Eliza. Not a place with angels sitting on clouds playing harps but one where there is peace and love and real life".
Eliza sensed that this was one of the reasons he had brought her here today on her Confirmation Day to show her that there were other ways of looking at things than through the eyes of the Church.

"Is that really what Heaven is?" she asked.
"That is how I see it, yes, but the people at your Church would not approve of my saying so" He began to look quite worried about this.
"Well I will not tell them that you said so" comforted Eliza.
Mac smiled at her childish innocence. If only life could always be so simple.

They walked on along the twisting paths and over bridges. Sometimes the bridges were over the river, sometimes over the canal and once over a railway line.

Suddenly the path opened out to become very wide and there straight ahead of her she saw Haigh Hall. She had never imagined any house could be so big or so beautiful.

"Do the people really live there?" she gasped incredulously.

"They certainly do and from what you tell me about your grandmother, it seems that you could have been living there too"

Eliza found this far too complicated to understand. It was all part of the mystery that her father never mentioned but which Aunt Lucy thought was so very important.

"I think we should go now Mac. I don't think I should really have come at all but now that I have seen the big house I would like to go home."

They turned towards the way they had come. Mac smiled to himself and thought he had been very clever in choosing Eliza's Confirmation Day to show her what might have been hers. He wanted her to have the confidence to rise above what might be her family's expectations for her and what indeed could be the lot of most women at that time.

Eliza was attending school in order to complete her own education, although she was to write later that she found the path to knowledge "indelicate, cruel and cold" particularly for little girls. Her schooldays were not happy; they were filled with tears and weariness and a longing for each day to end.

All this time, even more brothers were being born into that Millard home. At almost regular two yearly intervals, John, Charles, Edward and George were born. Eliza left school and began to work with her father. James Millard had expanded his interest in photography into a full time business. He had established a thriving studio where Eliza worked both as his assistant and his model. Being an extremely beautiful young woman, the pictures he took of her caused many a stir as he displayed them in his shop window. They attracted a great deal of custom also, as other young women wanted to prove that they could look just as beautiful as she did.

By this time, Mac had qualified as a doctor and was building up a practice for himself in the town. He had the reputation of never making a mistake, of never causing pain and of never allowing any of his patients to suffer needlessly. Throughout this time he never forsook Eliza, visiting her home whenever possible and talking for hours on end with her and her father.

James and Susannah could not help but like this wonderful godlike young man who so obviously idolised their daughter, but they were becoming increasingly concerned by the closeness of the relationship.

Eliza was nineteen years of age when the third daughter was born into the family. Beatrice was to be the one upon whom was to fall the duty of supporting the parents in their old age.

Mac's commitment to Atheism had now reached a new intensity and the local papers were filled with his writings and controversial views.
Eliza hung on his every word. Every time he wrote a letter to the local newspaper she sat and copied it out in her large untidy handwriting.
Mac was still in practice in the town but he spent many hours talking to groups of people about his views on religion. He also wrote many of his thoughts down for Eliza to read at her leisure. When they were talking together she understood everything he said but when he wrote his ideas down it was as if they were written by a different Mac, one who seemed far above Eliza and one whom she would have to strive hard to reach.
Nothing he wrote, whether for her or for anyone else, was ever discarded by Eliza. She knew that one day he would be famous and she would be the one who had stood by him when other people thought his ideas were strange and even wicked.

Her brothers were growing up too and were proving to be just as strong-minded as Eliza. Their father had high ambitions for all his children but although he believed that they should make their own success in whichever field attracted them, he did much to try to influence them if he sensed that they were being attracted into ways which did not meet with his approval. He supported them in their efforts when he felt able to do so but they often resented his support, sensing that there was a certain amount of patronage involved in its offering. Eliza was left very much to her own devices because James did not consider that she was likely to do anything which might prove too controversial. James was far-seeing enough to feel that being a woman did not preclude her from being successful and independent, although he assumed that she would follow the normal female paths to home and motherhood one day.

Eliza's brother James had already flown the nest and gone to set up a life for himself in the United States of America. Susannah knew that her flock had to be given its head but it was a sad day for her when she saw him go. She loved her children with an intense passion that she found difficult to describe, even to her husband and she would have longed to have tied young James to her and forbidden him to leave home. He and his father had exchanged angry words when it was realised that the boy had no intention of going into the family business. His father had longed for the Millard dynasty to prosper in the town but it was not to be. Young James yearned for an outdoor life and America seemed to be the place for him to succeed in farming.

Further heartache was to follow for Susannah. Alfred had begun to follow his father into the photographic business but was hindered by poor eyesight. He found his attempts at fulfilling his innate artistic urge through this medium to be frustrating and took instead to writing poetry. This delighted Eliza who saw in Alfred a soulmate. He was like his father in being able to master new tasks and concepts with remarkable ease, becoming at one point a skilled mechanic. Now he and his younger brother, William, decided that they too must go further afield to broaden their horizons. It was with a heavy heart that Susannah watched two more of her growing sons depart these shores and head for the United States. Alfred and William were not intent upon settling there; they began work on the Atlantic-Pacific Railway, Alfred as official photographer but turning his hand to engineering when the need arose and to soldiering when things got rough as they tended to do in those wild hostile days of Indian raids.

Eliza saw her brothers go and envied them their freedom. She never considered that her life would ever be with anyone other than Mac and none of the eligible young men who were attracted by her beauty could ever warrant even a second glance from her. Mac, however, was gaining both in popularity as a doctor and in notoriety as a preacher of atheism. He saw orthodox religion as merely another form of superstition or belief in the supernatural.

"I am convinced that superstition or supernaturalism is at the root of almost every ill that flesh is heir to" he wrote.

Eliza would question him on his writings, seeking only to understand and rarely wanting to argue with him. In her eyes he could neither do nor think any wrong.

"Do you really think that believing in God is like believing in Magic then?" she asked.

"Not exactly magic, Eliza. You see, most people think that the opinions and ideas are entirely their own. They think they have thought them up themselves. But if you think about it, they really only follow what their parents or friends consider to be the accepted patterns of behaviour or thought."
"Well that really is so" she thought, after a moment's consideration. "Our parents try to teach us what they think is right and we have enough respect for them to accept that".

"Exactly, and so that is how it goes on from generation to generation. Also we are aware that if we are to be accepted by society, we have to conform to the generally held views, whether these are about religion or anything else".

Eliza understood exactly what Mac meant and could relate this very much to her own life, to the way in which she was influenced by her father, a very strong-minded and in many ways unorthodox man himself. What Eliza did not seem to realise was that this influence was now being replaced by a different one, that of Mac.

"We are entering a new age now, Eliza, one in which we must start to get out of the shadows and emerge into the sunlight and freedom of nature and truth"

Mac had held these views for as long as he could remember. He felt certain that it was only fear and loyalty that caused people to hold on to the views of their parents and grandparents without question. Freedom of thought was considered almost immoral by some. He thought about the terms 'God' and 'Satan' and realised that what people did was attribute all good or moral deeds to God and all bad or immoral ones to Satan. It was an easy solution, an explanation which took all the burden of guilt from the individual.

"Do you say your prayers, Eliza?" Mac asked her one day.

"Only when I remember, I used to say the ones we learned in Sunday School when I was a child but now they seem a little childish"

"Do they get answered?" he asked.

"I don't really expect an answer, I don't think much about what I am praying for. Why are you asking me?"

"It is just that I have been thinking quite a lot recently about why people pray. I think they only pray about things they neither understand nor have any control over. For instance you would not pray that the sun would shine for twenty-four hours or that there would be an eclipse of the moon, because you understand the scientific reasons behind these events. The more knowledgeable people become, the less there will be for them to pray about".

Eliza listened with interest to all the views put forward by Mac and then thought carefully about them when she was alone. She never spoke about him to her family because she was not sure what their response might be. She could not bear to hear them criticise her beloved Mac and so for fear they might do so, she remained silent.

Criticism could not be avoided however when Mac began writing to the religious leaders in the town. He did this through the medium of the local newspaper. A long series of letters was published in that journal in which Mac emerged as a very literate and deep-thinking young man who felt so strongly about his principles that he ran the risk of being deserted by his patients, the very people on whom he depended for his livelihood.

This did not happen, however. His search throughout for Truth and Morality rendered him even more acceptable to the public than might have done a deeply religious belief. Many people saw sense in Mac's writings. He criticised the church leaders as being more concerned with getting money from the parishioners than in saving their souls. His patients knew this to be true in many cases and saw him as their saviour, putting in him the faith that he had convinced them should not be placed in a Supernatural God. There were others however, who did not share this confidence. As he passed by, men would call out 'Infidel' and even his faithful bull terrier, Nettle, was nicknamed 'Dr Macloghlin's unbeliever'. His surgery windows were smashed and every manner of abuse poured upon him by those who saw him only for his views and not for the good he did to his fellow men.

It hurt Eliza to see him treated in this way but it also convinced her and many others that he was right. It was the so-called Holy People, the upholders of religious belief in the 'Love of God' who had perpetrated the very deeds which to Eliza and Mac were the manifestations of evil.

Mac used his influence wherever he found it necessary. He had a remarkable gentleness with dogs and horses. He could tame the wildest thoroughbred, making it eager to join the Hunt and clearing what became known as 'The Macloghlin Jump'. However, he had soon had enough of following the hounds. He regarded it as nothing less than murder and this he could not countenance. His dedication was to the prolonging of life and this he practised with the resultant gratitude and love of the many that benefited from his touch.

Susannah kept her worries about Mac and Eliza very much to herself. She was well aware, from his attitude that James disapproved of the relationship, although he had not said very much about it so far.
She also knew that children did not always conform to their parents' wishes and that should the matter become a serious issue, then it might mean their losing Eliza forever.

Susannah's own grandparents had had to run the gauntlet of disapproval on religious grounds. Her grandfather had been a very devout Jew and her grandmother an Irish Protestant gentlewoman. She had been sixteen and he seventeen when they had married and they had remained Jew and Protestant. Their daughter Eliza also married young. She had been seventeen when Susannah was born and she had died sixteen months later. Susannah had no recollections of her own mother but had named her first child after her. She had hoped to be able to be the mother to Eliza that she missed so dreadfully herself. However, Eliza was her father's daughter; she loved her mother and the two were very close but in matters such as her relationship with Mac, Eliza would ask for no advice, she would please herself. Susannah wished that she herself could be so strong willed and could make decisions so easily. She knew she was of a generation of women who accepted their role in life.

Susannah knew that women were not considered to have valid thoughts or principles. In the matter of Eliza, as in most other things, James would decide what should be done and she would accept his decisions. She knew however, that if these decisions were opposed to Eliza's there would be angry words and Susannah's would be the tears to flow once more because of her love for her children.

CHAPTER 2

Mac still lived in his parents' house, a very grand affair by local standards. It stood some miles from the town centre in the small village of Haigh. The occupants of Haigh Hall could often be seen out riding and sometimes they would attend morning service at the village church directly opposite the Macloghin home, Culraven House.

Eliza was twenty-one years of age when her youngest brother Victor was born and she began to have thoughts of moving out of the family home and seeking some independence. Margaret had left school and was helping out at home with the housework and caring for the younger members of the family. Eliza still dreamed of marrying Mac and cherished little girl fantasies of the dress and the long walk down the aisle. Mac would be waiting for her and the heads of the congregation would turn as she approached to the strains of the wedding march. There would be gasps at her beauty which on that day would be even greater than usual because now she and Mac were to be joined for Eternity.

As a photographer she often had to help to take the photographs of wedding groups. This was the modern way to do things. After the wedding, the party would go to the Studio where the often tedious and painstaking procedure would be undertaken. However, anyone who could afford to have photographs taken in this way did so, in order to commit the moment to posterity. The pictures hung on drawing room walls or stood on top of pianos and almost always the composition was the same; the bride seated along with the bridesmaids, the groom and best man standing behind them. Sometimes the picture was only of the bride and groom but occasionally the entire family was included. Eliza thought that she could tell a great deal about a family from the way things went at these sessions. If the mother-in-law took charge she felt the marriage was doomed from the start.

It was after one such session, as Eliza was seeing the wedding party out to their carriage that Mac appeared at the door. He had never done this before and Eliza was surprised to see him there.

"I would like you to take my portrait, Eliza." He said.

"You Mac? But why?" Eliza wondered whether he was teasing her or not.

"I feel that a doctor should have a portrait of himself to hang on the wall of his consulting room so that the patients can see him to be a person of worth."

This convinced Eliza that he was teasing her. Mac was the last person in the world to consider himself to be a 'person of worth'. His entire philosophy was built around his belief in equality.

"I see." She decided to go along with his pretence "so that people will talk about 'the Great Macloghlin' and will shower you with gifts?"

"Exactly so, Eliza," he teased, "No actually, I really do want a portrait of myself but not for those reasons. Some of the poetry I have written over the years is to be collected into a book and the compiler thought it would be a good idea to have a picture of me inside the frontispiece. So that those who read the book can see what an incredibly handsome fellow I am." They both laughed and Eliza loved him with all her heart. She was pleased that he had come to her with this important commission.

"If you come back tomorrow at two o'clock in the afternoon, I think we might be able to arrange the matter for you, Sir" Eliza kept a straight face.

Mac thanked her politely and left the shop. For a moment she wondered whether he had misconstrued her formality and then she remembered the way they had laughed together and she consoled herself with the fact that he was far too intelligent and sensitive to be upset by her girlish whims.

18

Nevertheless for the rest of the day Eliza went about her tasks with little awareness of her surroundings. She loved Mac with such an intense passion that she felt she would die if he were to leave her.

That evening she sat in her room and wrote in her diary:

'Mac, my life would be over without you. I know that even Death could not steal you from me. Return, my love and let us scale the heights of love together'

She closed her diary and laid it carefully in her drawer. Then she left her room and made her way down the stairs and to the drawing room. As she approached, she heard voices from inside, angry voices and the sound of her mother weeping. She opened the door with some trepidation, half expecting to be told to leave as this did not concern her.

Her mother was sitting in her usual place by the fireside with the baby in her arms. James, Eliza's father, was standing at the window, looking out. As Eliza entered the room her turned and came towards her. His face was drawn and there was a look that Eliza had never seen before.

"Eliza, you are twenty-one now and a woman" her father began, "however there is much talk in the town about your attending meetings addressed by young Macloghlin".

"Yes father, you know that I like to go to listen to Mac whenever it is possible, but why does it now seem to surprise you?"

James was obviously trying hard to choose his words prudently. He did not want to anger his daughter; neither did he think he should allow the situation to continue.

"Eliza, please" he stretched out his arms towards Eliza, "you know we love you and we want you to be happy but we also want you to be respected by the people in the town. We are business people and any hint of scandal could mean the end of our prosperity".

"Scandal? To what do you refer, father? I have done nothing to create a scandal and neither has Mac"

"You are so innocent, Eliza" her father began.

"I am innocent of anything improper, if that is what you are implying". Eliza was becoming angry. She began to pace the room in a decidedly unladylike manner and Susannah knew that stormy times were ahead.

"Eliza dear, your father is only trying to help" Susannah intervened.

Both James and Eliza turned on Susannah. She felt like the little girl in the corner – what chance had she against two Millards.

"Mother, please keep out of this, it is a matter for my father and me".

Her father turned round at this and Eliza thought she had never seen him so angry. His face contorted, he thumped with his fist on the table. Eliza trembled.

Susannah got up from her chair and weeping silently took her baby son away from the scene.

James appeared not to have noticed his wife's departure. He continued "I have read the letters in the local paper, written by Macloghlin and I must admit I agree with much of what he says. I think he has a large band of followers and he certainly is a very clever man. However I am told that he is speaking more and more against the principle of marriage. Whatever he thinks about God and the Church is his business but once he talks about free love and people living together without being married, then that is another matter altogether."

"But what has that to do with me, father?"

James looked at Eliza and realised that she really was as innocent as he had hoped. She saw no connection between what Mac preached and her own relationship with him.

"Eliza do you not see? The scoundrel does not believe in marriage. You are seen to be his close friend, his disciple even, surely you see that people will begin to imagine that the two of you are living in sin. I heard the way the two of you were laughing together in the studio today. This is more than a passing friendship."

Now Eliza understood. It was what people thought that mattered to her parents, not what was actually happening. They knew she was not living with Mac, but worried that people might think she was. Surely they knew that he still lived in his parents' home. His letters to the local newspaper were always headed with that address.

Then another thought occurred to Eliza, one that made her wonder why it had not occurred before. Mac had sometimes talked about being with her and she had always thought this meant they would be married, but now she knew why he had never actually mentioned marriage.

Eliza needed to be alone, to consider all the implications of her father's words. She excused herself and went to her room.

Susannah heard Eliza go upstairs and followed. Gently she tapped on the door and whispered "Eliza, would you like to talk to me about this?"

She opened the door very slowly and peered round and into the room. Eliza was sitting in a chair, gazing into space.

"Oh mother, why does everything have to start going wrong like this?"
"Nothing has started to go wrong, that is what your father is trying to avoid"
"I know that but obviously he does not trust my judgement. He thinks I cannot make decisions by myself."
"I think you are quite wrong, Eliza. I think he knows only too well that you can and do make decisions for yourself. He is merely concerned that those decisions might be ones you could regret."

"I want to share my life with Mac. I had always thought we would be married one day but now I realise that that will never be. I have listened to him preaching his views on marriage but in a strange way I never thought about it affecting us"

"Has he never discussed marriage or your lives together?"

"No, we always seem to talk about ideals and philosophies and never about our personal lives".

Susannah did not know whether she should be pleased or sorry about this. If they had never discussed the question then this probably meant that Mac did not consider it a possibility. On the other hand he might be biding his time, waiting until Eliza was so deeply under his spell that she would agree with whatever he suggested. Susannah was horrified when she realised that she was thinking in exactly the same way that James did.

"Your father loves you and he does not want to see you hurt. If you did go to live with this man without being married to him, then you would cause such a scandal that none of us would be able to hold up our heads in the town again. Think what that would do to his practice. People would not want to be seen visiting or being visited by a doctor with such a reputation."

"But mother, people know his views already and they have not deserted him."

"Not everyone knows his views, apart from those who go to hear him speak and those who read the newspapers. Most of those who go to listen to him agree with him already or they go to argue. Also, people often find it easy to accept someone's views in theory, when that is all they seem to be; but when they are seen to affect their lives; well that is sometimes a different matter"

"I am glad you came to talk to me mother. I cannot talk with father when he is angry. It makes me angry too and we both say thinks we regret later".

Susannah felt happier than she had done for some time. She left her daughter and quietly returned to the kitchen.

Eliza washed her face and went downstairs. Her father was still sitting in the drawing room.

"I am sorry father. I know you are only concerned for my well-being. I have thought over what you said and I can assure you that no matter what people might think, I have no intention of living with Mac yet, whether married or unmarried. I hope you will not think unkindly of me father, but I have been thinking quite a lot recently about finding a little house of my own and learning to look after myself. There are quite enough of you in this house and one less would only help matters. If you could allow me to have a small wage for working in the studio then I am sure that if I found a modest house to rent I could easily manage".

James wondered why she had suddenly become so much more amenable, but he assumed his words had influenced her. He was not happy about her new proposals but he also knew they were the only ones he was going to hear. He had never been faced with the question of paying his own family before and he did not know how to deal with this suggestion. He had always thought that his children would stand by him and help him to make a success of the studio.

That night Eliza slept badly. She had to sort out in her mind what her next moves should be. Should she discuss this with Mac or should she make all her plans and then tell him about them? Would he admire her or condemn her for her decision to live alone?

The following afternoon Mac came to the studio as arranged. Aunt Lucy was there and ignorant of the previous evening's events, made a great fuss of him. Eliza smiled to herself, thinking that Aunt Lucy could not possibly be aware of Mac's views, or of the rumours, otherwise she would not have touched him with a barge pole. She was far too concerned with public opinion to let her heart rule her head.

Mac was dressed for the occasion in a light brown suit. His hair gleamed and his moustache was carefully groomed. He sat in the chair and looked on admiringly as the two women handled the technical equipment necessary for the portrait. The background had to be just right and the lighting perfect before the camera could be brought into play.

When the picture had been taken, Aunt Lucy left them alone while she went to see to some more clients. Mac looked at Eliza and asked "Is something troubling you?"

Eliza wished that her feelings were not quite so apparent. She knew there was no point in lying to Mac, he was far too perceptive.
"Well, I had a slight disagreement with my parents last evening and it has left me quite saddened."
"Is it something you can discuss with me, or is it private, family business?"
Eliza wondered what to answer and then she spoke quietly so that Aunt Lucy could not hear.
"My father is concerned about our relationship. He thinks that people who know your views about marriage might think we are living in sin together".
Mac threw back his head and laughed loudly at this. Eliza felt like a little girl again when she had said something silly and Mac laughed at her childishness. Was it such impossibility to him that he should react in this manner? Mac looked at her solemn face and immediately realised how he had hurt her. "Oh Eliza, please forgive me. I did not mean to be rude, but it is your choice of words 'Living in sin' - they are such inappropriate words".
"Well, you know what I mean" she said, "that is how people are described if they live together without being married"

"Oh Eliza, I know that, but that is precisely why it is so inappropriate. I have spent so long in trying to come to terms with the ideal of marriage that I am convinced that the whole concept is both untruthful and unfounded. It is the ones who are married who are the sinful ones. One day my theories will not seem so outrageous. They will be accepted among people who think about the matter rather than accepting the traditional views without question. Do you remember what we said about people just accepting the views of their parents about religion in general rather than formulating their own ideas?"

Eliza gazed at him with her eyes wide and he thought back to the little girl he had first seen so many years ago. He had known many young ladies over the years. While he had been a doctor he had had many opportunities to form relationships with women of his own age, but there was something almost hypnotic about Eliza. It was not just her beauty, although he had to admit that he had watched that mature over the years and he felt rather like a gardener who had cultivated an exotic plant. Just as that gardener would hate to allow anyone else to tend his precious plant, he must be the only one. One day that beauty would fade but he would have enjoyed every moment of it while it lasted.

Mac faced her and took her upturned face in his hands. He placed a gently kiss on her forehead, on her nose and finally fully on her lips.

"I will never want to marry you, Eliza, at least not in the legal sense. What is marriage anyway other than a legal contract? We do not need that. Marriage is an indissoluble contract which can only be terminated either by death or dishonour".

He knew in his heart that he could commit himself to Eliza for the rest of his life but there were other reasons why he did not want such a contract, reasons which Mac kept locked away in his innermost soul, which he would never divulge to a soul, least of all to Eliza.

"But Mac, I would never want to break such a contract with you" Eliza wanted desperately to understand and agree with Mac but she felt that he was saying something that she did not want to hear.

Eliza ached to be able to tell understand and agree with what was going on inside that brilliant brain and Mac pleaded with his eyes for her to do so.

"Just think of the marriage ceremony, Eliza" he said, "it says 'I will' How can anyone say that? One can say 'I do love' but to love is beyond the power or domain of will; no one can or ought to say 'I will'. It goes on about the Law 'making her his'. I do not desire to make any woman mine; it must be her love for me and mine for her which can alone dictate the relationship between us. Where there is that love, any other form of bond, such as a legal contract is as insulting as it is unnecessary. Where that love does not exist, any contract is as untruthful as it is immoral."

"I think your father is right" he went on, "if people thought we were living together without being married, then it would cause a great scandal. This world, and particularly this town, is not ready for such things. No, Eliza, we must remain friends as we are now and then one day, when the time is right we will be together for ever, I promise you."
Eliza was too ashamed to tell Mac that she would feel cheated out of the big day and the bridal dress. He would regard this as feminine weakness. She decided not to tell Mac any of her other plans. He had made her very happy and she did not want anything to break the spell she was under at that moment.
"I really must return to my work" she said, "there are other clients waiting you know"
"None others waiting for you, I hope." He held out his arms and Eliza went to him. Hiding her face against his rough coat, she shed tears that he could not see. Mac would want her to be strong at this time and not give way to selfish emotions.

Eliza thought afterwards that this was probably the moment when she realised that she would do anything Mac wanted. If he wanted them to jump off the edge of the world together she would do it. They held each other close for some time without speaking and then when she knew she was sufficiently composed to do so, she pulled away from him.

Eliza spent the next few days making plans for her future. She was aware that she had committed herself to a venture which would not be easy but from which there was no turning back. Now that she knew that Mac would not want to marry her, she realised that she had to plan a life of her own. If Mac wished them to remain friends then she needed to be independent in order that her parents did not question her every move.

She wondered how she should set about finding a house for herself. She had never had to be concerned with such matter; few women had, but she had made the decision and formulated a plan to put it into practice.

One of the regular clients at the studio was a wealthy business man who owned quite a lot of property in the town. She decided to pay him a visit and seek his advice.

She had spoken to nobody about her decision to visit Mr Larchworth and she left home that day without giving anyone the details of her business.

Stepping up to the door of the big house, she almost felt like turning back but she thought of all that would mean and taking her courage in both hands, she rang the bell. A neatly dressed maid servant opened the door.

"Yes Ma'am?" she asked.

"I am Miss Millard, a business acquaintance of your employer, could you please ask if he could spare me a few moments?"

"Please come inside and I will tell him you are here" she said

Eliza stood inside the splendid entrance hall and took in the whole scene; the magnificent pictures, the bronze sculptures, the rich carpets, everything tastefully chosen. Eliza decided there and then that one day she would own a house like this.

The maid servant returned and ushered Eliza into a drawing room which was elegantly furnished and yet seemed to glow with a warm welcome. She was quite surprised to see some framed photographs of Mr Larchworth adorning the sideboard. They were the ones Eliza herself had taken.

Mr Larchworth came forward to greet her; he was obviously delighted at her visit.

"Miss Millard, what a pleasure this is! Of course it is always a pleasure to be in your company but for you to visit me in my home, well it is really more than I can comprehend. I feel quite humble".

Eliza was somewhat taken aback by the warmth of his welcome; she had met him on several occasions in the studio but she had never realised that he had given her more than a second glance. Such was Eliza's naivety that it had never occurred to her until now that it was unusual for a man to require quite so many pictures of himself and now she reflected on it she had taken several over the past year or so.

"I really need to ask your advice and possibly your help".
Her coat was taken and the maid servant dismissed with orders to bring afternoon tea. Eliza was invited to sit alongside Mr Larchworth on the sumptuous settee.
"Well I am only too pleased you came, whatever the reason."
Eliza took a deep breath and began – "I know you own some property in the town and I wondered whether there might be a small cottage which you would be willing to rent to me."

Eliza looked at him and knew that her request would be difficult for him to comprehend. Young women did not leave home and live by themselves unless they had no alternative. Eliza had a good home and her parents were fairly well off. Had there been some family disagreement, he wondered, which had resulted in her being asked to leave?

"Would you be living by yourself?" he asked.

Eliza wondered whether he had heard the local gossip, whether he thought the house was for her to share with Mac.

"At present I have not made any definite plans" she explained, "but I feel that I need to be independent. I have a good career in my father's business but I would like the chance to care for myself at this time – that is it, no more or less."

Mr Larchworth was not entirely sure that this was the whole story but he was happy to turn a blind eye to the details if it was going to give him the opportunity to see more of this fascinating young woman. He had been quite obsessed by her from the first time he saw her and if it had meant having numerous photographs taken of himself in order to be in her company then that was what he had had to do.

Afternoon tea was served and he took advantage of the break in the conversation to decide how he might best respond.

"Are you anxious to obtain this property immediately?" he asked.

"As soon as possible; I am very excited at the prospect and I cannot wait to begin my new life."

"Well I can think of one particularly suitable property, but I would have to make a few enquiries first. Can you call back tomorrow afternoon and I will let you know for certain." His heart raced at the prospect of her calling again. He wondered how long he could keep her waiting for the property in order to see even more of her.

"That is very kind of you, Mr Larchworth, I will call back at the same time tomorrow and then if you have not been able to find anything for me I will have to start looking elsewhere. I came to you first of all because I regarded you as someone I could trust, but perhaps you could suggest someone else who could help me if you are not able to,"

Mr Larchworth was not going to hand over this lady to anyone else. He knew he could help her but he needed to prolong this part of the transaction.

"Oh do not worry about that. I am sure I can find something suitable for you" he assured her.

Eliza's coat was brought and he helped her on with it. As he did so he let his hands linger on her shoulders and felt the warmth of her young body beneath his fingers. He wanted this lady more than he had ever wanted anything and usually what he wanted he usually got.
Eliza began to understand how this man felt and she understood that she could use this to get anything she wanted from him. She had never before felt such feelings of power.

He saw her to the door and watched as she walked off along the street.

That evening Eliza returned home in a much more settled frame of mind. She knew that her decision to leave home would cause heartache within the family but she was determined to make a success of it.
When she arrived home her mother asked where she had been.
"I went to visit a friend" she replied.
"Oh yes, which friend that might be?" her mother persisted.
"Mother, I do not need to explain where I am going and where I have been every time I go in or out of the house" Eliza was immediately sorry for speaking so to her mother but she was so weary of this constant questioning. Her brothers had left home; no one knew where they were or what they were doing, so they could not be cross-questioned in this way.
"Please allow me to have my own life, mother" Eliza pleaded.

Susannah shrugged, hurt that Eliza felt unable to confide in her. She knew inside that there was something wrong. Whenever her children had problems she knew it almost before they did. While her sons had been abroad, she had been in constant touch with them through her feelings and sometimes she found this power a decided disadvantage. Many times she would waken up during the night feeling anxious and afraid that there was something wrong. Sometimes she never found out what it had been, but on other occasions she would receive a message or a visit which would explain the anxiety to her. She knew that life would be so much simpler for her if she was able to distinguish the good signs from the bad. This time she knew for certain that they were bad. Problems lay ahead that she felt she could not control. Susannah wished that when her children had left her womb, they had not left that little part of themselves behind which caused her to take all of their worries upon herself.

Eliza wanted desperately to share her news with someone and would have loved to talk to her mother; however she knew that Susannah would be deeply hurt at losing her and decided it would be more prudent to wait until she had something more definite to confide. She went to her room and lay on her bed. She had lain there so many times over the years, thinking about Mac and longing for the time when they would be together. She thought of her brothers. She thought of Alfred off travelling the world with William. They had no interest at all in their eccentric older sister. Little had been heard of James since he went to America, farming it was assumed. Out of sight out of mind, she often thought. The others were too young to understand anyway and by the time they grew up, attitudes might have changed and they would forgive her. Forgive her! Why did she think she would need forgiveness? She lay there until she fell asleep. She dreamed of walking through rose scented gardens with Mac. People were pointing their fingers at them and whispering behind their hands. The two lovers clung to each other and then people started to pull them apart. They reached out for each other but soon the others were too strong for them and they felt themselves being torn away from each other and Eliza heard someone shout "He's not fit to be a doctor if he can't behave decently". Another shouted "he'll not touch my wife again. He can't be trusted with women."

Suddenly Eliza was awake, her heart pounding. The nightmare was over, or was it? Had she imagined those voices or were people really saying such things about them?

Mac had worked for so long to qualify and build a reputation for himself as a brilliant and caring doctor and any scandal would mean the end of it all. There was truth in the dream. Rightly or wrongly, no one would want to be treated by him if this was the way he was thought to be living.

Eliza slept fitfully for the rest of the night and awoke feeling far from refreshed in the morning. She poured water from the bedroom jug into the bowl and splashed her face with it. She put on a clean dress and brushed her hair. Then she went down to breakfast where she knew she had to face her family alone.

The faces that looked up as she entered the room gave no sign as to their feelings. Margaret, at thirteen thought the sun shone from her older sister and hoped that she might grow up to be just as beautiful. She thought that although Mac was rather old, he was still quite handsome. She recognised the signs of stress in both her parents and Eliza but was not sure of the cause. Ten year old John concentrated hard on his breakfast and his only concern was how soon he could get back to the picture he was drawing for his mother's birthday. Charles, Edward and George were too young to be concerned with much other than their games and baby Beatrice at just two years old just sat and smiled at everyone. Eliza saw them all and knew that though she loved them dearly, her love for Mac was of a different kind.

She went over to her father and kissed him on his forehead. "Good morning, father" she said "whatever you might think, I really do love you very much."

James looked up from his morning paper and removed his spectacles. "I never doubted that. Eliza but it seems this fellow has more influence over you than I do."

"That is not fair". Eliza's eyes flashed in anger. "I have discussed the matter with him and it would appear that you are right. He does not want to marry me."

James laughed with the kind of self-satisfied laugh that made Susannah cringe.

"I think we all knew that already"

"Neither does he wish us to live together and he agrees with you that much damage might be done both to your business and to his practice if this silly gossip were allowed to escalate".

Eliza decided to make the most of her moment in the limelight; she would keep her father waiting. James looked apprehensive. She glanced at herself in the mirror over the mantelpiece, saw that she was still presenting the correct image and went on;

"I have given the matter much thought and I have decided that we both have too much to lose by allowing our reputations to suffer as you think they might."

"Well I am glad to hear that. I think you should think about finding a young man who is established in a profession and who is ready to marry and settle down. Macloghlin is too full of theories and fancies to make a decent husband for you."

"Oh, you misunderstand me father," explained Eliza, "I have no intention of marrying anyone else. Edward Macloghlin is the only man I will ever love. He is the one I want to share my life with. I said he did not wish us to live together, I should have added 'just yet'"

Susannah looked towards her husband and all the panic which had filled her since the previous day left her. Now that she knew what was

33

happening she was much calmer. Perhaps there was still time for Eliza to change her mind, since there were no immediate plans.

"but at the moment," Eliza went on, " I prefer to do as I suggested the other night. I am going to find a little house for myself and I am going to learn to look after myself."

James sighed deeply and got up from the table. He had raised a daughter to be independent of thought and now that independence was causing him this heartache. He was angry and hurt but he knew he did not want to lose her.
"I see"
"Are you going to trust my judgement in future, father?" she asked.
"We shall see, we shall see." He said quietly as he left the room.

Eliza turned to her mother. "I hope that it will not make you too sad when I leave home"
"Eliza, it is your life and you must live it as you see fit. I chose to marry and have a husband and family. Perhaps if I had had your opportunities life would have been very different for me. I wish you well. I will always be there to pick up the pieces, you will always be my daughter, my first child and I will be with you in spirit whatever happens." The tears welled up once more and Susannah tried to hide them from Eliza. Surely this strong-willed daughter of hers would not want a mother who cried so easily. Eliza rushed to her mother and cradled her in her arms. They wept together for some minutes and knew that the bond they shared would never be broken.

The next afternoon Eliza kept her appointment as planned. She had hardly been able to contain her excitement at the prospect of hearing Mr Larchworth tell her that he had found her a house and that she could move into it as soon as she wished. Her confidence was much greater as she arrived for this second visit. This time she knew she would be well received. The maid admitted her to where Mr Larchworth was waiting. He stood up as she entered and came towards her with outstretched hands.

"My dear Miss Millard, Eliza, may I call you Eliza?"

Eliza nodded and smiled warmly at him. How could she refuse his request when she was so eagerly awaiting his news?
"I have made enquiries and I think I have just the house for you".
Eliza's heart skipped.
He went on, "I thought it would be a good idea if we took a short walk there now. It is not far away and you could see for yourself whether you think it suitable or not."
"I would be delighted, that is if you are sure you have the time,"she said eagerly.

He put on his coat and hat and they stepped out together from his front door. He offered her his arm and together they passed down the street, turning the corner just a few doors away from his own house. They had hardly walked any distance at all when he stopped in front of two small steps leading up to the front door of a small terraced house. Taking a key from his pocket he opened the door and led Eliza directly into the front room. The house was small compared with her parents' house and against Mr Larchworth's it was positively tiny but this room was surprisingly large. A bay window looked directly on to the street so that passers-by could look right into the room. Now Eliza realised the need for curtains at the window. He showed her into the room at the back of the house. This had a large black fire grate with an oven. Eliza imagined herself cooking meals for Mac on the fire. The scullery at the back of this room had a flat stone sink and some shelves on the wall. The window looked out on to a tiny back yard with a small patch of grass. A rose tree climbed up the rough brick wall at the end of the garden and there was a wooden gate leading into a passageway which ran behind the row of houses. She saw that there was an outside toilet at the bottom of the yard and a coal shed. Upstairs there were two small bedrooms.

However small the house might be, Eliza saw it as her path to freedom. She would not always live in such a house. One day she and Mac would live in a magnificent home like Mr Larchworth's. She turned and beamed at him.

"Oh, Mr Larchworth!" she cried
"Please call me Thomas, I am sure we know each other well enough for that"
"Oh Thomas, this is wonderful, but what is the rent? I never thought to indicate how much, or indeed how little, I could afford"

He thought briefly about this. He had to be sure that the rent was low enough for her to afford but not so low as to make her suspect his motives for wanting her here.

"Would two shillings a week be too much?" he asked tentatively.
"No indeed, that would be more than reasonable, I am sure I can afford that."

She had no idea how much her father would be willing to pay her but she sincerely hoped that he considered her worth much more than two shillings a week.
"I cannot wait to move into this house" she said excitedly but I will need to obtain some furniture before I can do that."
"I hope you will not be offended by this suggestion, Eliza, but in my house there is a great deal of furniture which I will never use. Some of it has been bought at auctions and is merely stored there until a buyer can be found. I would be only too pleased to allow you the use of some of that until such time as you are able to purchase your own. Whenever you decide to leave the house, the furniture can stay where it is. In that way I am merely storing it for myself".

Eliza thought this a very generous offer. She realised now that she had been carried away by her enthusiasm to leave home and she had never given a thought to how she would pay for furniture. In fact she was embarrassed to think what she would have done had he not made this suggestion to her.

They walked back to the big house round the corner and Thomas showed her through the many rooms filled with the most magnificent pieces of furniture. Although most of it would be far too big for the tiny rooms in her new house, occasionally Thomas would stop and point out something small enough and suitable for her use.
Soon they had selected enough pieces to set Eliza up in her home. There was even a very elegant bed with a mahogany headboard which he insisted would fit into the largest of her bedrooms. It already had on it a thick feather mattress which Thomas assured her had hardly ever been used. By the time they had finished the two of them were giggling as though they had known each other for years and Eliza thought what a very good friend Thomas had turned out to be.

Her father and mother were sitting together when she arrived home. Her father was smoking his pipe and her mother knitting as she always seemed to be. They looked up as she entered the room.

"Listen, Eliza", her father began, "I am sorry we had that little disagreement. I hope you and I can still be friends".
"Father," she chose her words carefully, "I love you dearly but I have to make my own decisions now. I am no longer a child and you will have to trust me".
"How can you possibly make decisions for yourself? You are only a girl; you know nothing of the world and the ways of men. This fellow only wants you for the prestige it will give him over his friends. All of their wives are probably fat and ugly and to walk out with a beautiful young girl like you on his arm will give him quite an edge upon the others".

Eliza was horrified. What did her father think she was? A strumpet who was there to be used by men and then cast aside?

"If you want to continue to live under my roof then you must abide by my rules", her father shouted.

She cringed at the anger in his voice but refused to become intimidated by it.

"Then I am afraid that I cannot do that. I have already indicated to you that I would like to find a place of my own. In fact, I have done just that. As soon as I can make the arrangements I will be leaving your house, as you call it. It will be sad for me to leave but I have to think of my own life and how I wish to spend it".

"You are not thinking at all, Eliza. How do you propose to live? I certainly have no intention of keeping you. Once you leave this house you must look after yourself."

"But father, what about my work at the studio. Surely that deserves some small payment."

"You have been paid more than adequately by being kept here. A comfortable home and good food on the table are more than ample reward. Your clothes have been bought for you and I must say they have always been the best money could buy".

"But surely father, you can see that we are constantly quarrelling. I need to leave this house and then perhaps we will be able to meet and work together more amicably".

James was not listening. He went on, stabbing his finger at her with every word.

"What kind of security will you have? When he grows tired of you or finds a younger, more beautiful girl than you, he will not hesitate to throw you out on the streets. Then you will come crying back here, pleading forgiveness and expecting me to have you back. Well understand this, young lady, once you leave, you never return to live under this roof. Is that understood?"

Eliza could not believe that her father was saying such things to her. He obviously believed that she was planning to live with Mac and she was not going to try to persuade him otherwise. He did not trust her to make good judgements and although the tears ached behind her eyes she refused to give into them.

She looked over his shoulder to where her mother sat, ashen-faced, afraid to utter a word when her husband was in such an angry mood.
"What do you think, mother," she asked, "would you never allow me to return either?"
Susannah trembled inwardly. Her lips quivered and she attempted to speak.
"Please, James, please don't be so ...." she began, but her words were cut short as James spun round upon his wife.
"This is nothing to do with you, don't interfere".

Eliza's heart went out to her mother. Here was a woman who had devoted more than half her life to this man and their children. She was a woman with a brain which she was not allowed to use, feelings she was not allowed to express. She loved her children with an intensity that at that time Eliza was unable to comprehend.

Susannah had been as intoxicated by James as Eliza now was by Mac. Against her own father's wishes she had married him at a very early age and had devoted herself to him. She had long since lost touch with her own hopes for herself because she thought only of what James would like or what would be the best for the children. Many were the times when she thought that she would prefer not to have any more children but always James' will prevailed and another would be on the way. When the children were younger he was the one to decide how they should be brought up and because he was a little older than she, she gave in to what she imagined must be the wisdom of maturity. As the boys grew older and began to question their father's ideas and policies, she tried to influence him into trying to see their points of view. Sometimes angry scenes such as the present one with Eliza would ensue. At other times he would turn his back on the situation and the boys would do what they wanted to do. These were the times

Susannah dreaded because sooner or later James would turn on her and blame her for not supporting him.

"Why will you not allow my mother to have a mind of her own?" Eliza pleaded.

"This has nothing to do with your mother. She is like you, a woman who can't be expected to understand the way men's minds work. She would support you whatever you wanted to do because she is afraid you might go away and she could not live with that."

Eliza was furious. "Father, I cannot believe that you mean these terrible things. My brothers left because they could not please you and now you are trying to drive me away as well."

"Absolute nonsense" shouted James, "you are the one who wants to desert us. If that is the way you feel then it would probably be as well if you did go off with Macloghlin. Let us see whether he will let you please yourself or not".

Susannah felt the tears start to overflow and she knew she had to be strong. She turned her attention once more to her knitting but could only think that this man was doing it again. He had to have his own way in every aspect of their lives. Her love for her children was the only thing she had that he could not take away and even that was being destroyed. Eliza had been quite right; Alfred, James and William had had their own ideas and he had not allowed them to voice them. He knew what he wanted for his sons. He wanted them to have respectable professional lives so that he could talk about them with his friends and feel proud of them. He was still proud of them up to a point. He heard from them occasionally and wherever they went people seemed to respect them, but they were not here where Susannah could see and touch them. She wondered how much longer her life would go on like this. She was still only thirty-nine years of age, a young woman by most standards and yet she had eleven children. Her figure was gone and her hair was already turning grey. She had nothing of her own but then neither did most women in her position. She belonged to James. He had 'made her his' and she must abide by that. She thought of Mac who wanted Eliza to share his life without the legal ties of marriage and although she would never dare to utter these thoughts to James, she half agreed with him. Why should a woman be shackled thus to a man?

Susannah realised with horror that the tears she had tried to hide were falling anyway, soaking her knitting. Her shoulders heaved with silent sobs and Eliza was kneeling at her feet trying to comfort her. She held her mother's hand tightly to her lips.

"Father, my mother has suffered for love of you; I have no intention of suffering in the same manner. If for no other reason than that, I will never marry".

The hurt showed on James's face and Susannah recognised it. She knew however that the hurt was for himself and anger that his daughter should think about him in this way, not hurt for his wife.

"How dare you speak to me like this", he shouted at Eliza, "as I have said already, you are just a girl and have no experience of the world. You should realise that the only important thing in any woman's life is to have a good husband who can provide her with a home in which to raise a family".
Susannah felt herself becoming more and more angry.

"James, Eliza does not need to do as I did. She is of a new generation of women who expect more from life than I did and she is not being ungracious or disrespectful to you".
"Will you stop taking Eliza's side against me, woman." For a moment she thought he would strike her but he calmed down enough for Eliza to venture a second time with her argument.

"Father, mother is entitled to her own opinions. If they happen to disagree with yours, then you must accept that, but you cannot deny her having them".

"A woman's place is to support her husband at all times. She cannot have differing opinions from his".

As James spoke, he saw his daughter relax her grip on her mother's hand.

"Thank you, father" smiled Eliza, "you have just expressed the very reasons why I do not intend to become a married woman".

"The reason you will not be married is because that fellow does not want to marry you. He thinks he can have his cake and his ha'penny too. All this talk about his theories of marriage is pure nonsense. He just does not want to make a commitment".

Eliza hoped that her mother would not suffer for speaking up for her in this way. She was certain that James would insist that had Susannah supported him, Eliza would never have left home. She knew now, more than ever, that she could not remain at home any longer than was necessary.

"Father, when I first came into this room, I told you that although I love you I must make my own decisions. However I would be much happier if I felt that I had your support."

"I do not appear to have anyone's support, myself". James slumped in his chair and Eliza's heart filled with sympathy for him. She knelt at his feet and looked up into his face.

"I only ask you to trust me father. I will never disgrace you if you can find it in your heart to let me live my life as I see fit".

"The way you see fit will lead to total disgrace but it is evident that I have no influence over you whatsoever."

Eliza turned and swept out of the room.

Susannah stood in her kitchen and thought about Eliza's proposals. There was no doubt in her mind that she would miss her daughter if she left home but she had known that one day she would leave to start a family of her own. She also knew that with her gone there would be fewer scenes such as she had just endured. Looking on the practical side, Eliza's room could be used for Margaret who was reaching an age when she needed a room of her own. There were in fact several advantages in agreeing to pay Eliza a small wage. She would have to provide her own clothes and James had been right in commenting upon the cost of these. This in itself would constitute a large saving. Once Susannah had composed herself and formulated her argument, she decided to return and face James.

He was still sitting where she had left him, his face filled with misery. Where had he gone wrong? He asked himself. He had tried to be a good father; he knew what was right for his family but they all appeared to resent him for it. It all hinged on Susannah. They would always listen to her rather than to him and if he opposed her they sprang immediately to her defence.

He hardly looked up as she entered the room. She sat at his feet, just as Eliza had done and his hand went out to stroke her hair. Where had the years gone and their hopes for their family? What had their own love become? The centre of a battlefield with broken hearts scattered around. But whose hearts? His and Susannah's most of all. She loved her children and could not bear to lose them and he knew this was not how it should be. Even her sons had tried to tell her that it was wrong and that she must let them leave the nest.
"James dear" she began hesitantly, "I have been thinking about Eliza…"
"And I suppose you think I am a wicked, tyrannical father, imposing my will on the children again – well you deal with this anyway you like – I want no further part in the matter".

"James, love, you cannot do that. Yours are the decisions which count, not mine. I think you are a wonderful father and a dear, dear husband but sometimes you need to listen a little more. Eliza is right, she would be better away from here, much as it would break my heart. She is sensible and mature and could become even more so if she had the opportunity. I had three children when I was her age and I had no parents to shelter me. Perhaps when she has to support herself she will appreciate us rather more".

Several times, while Susannah was speaking, James tried to interrupt her but she was determined to say what she had planned and each time he tried to speak, she put her finger firmly on his lips.

"How can I afford to pay her enough to live on?"
"If she leaves the studio, which I am sure she will do if you refuse to pay her a wage, you will have to pay an assistant. Then there is another point: we will have a little more room in this house."

James sighed. He knew that everything Susannah had said was true. He just did not want to appear to have lost the battle.

"All right then, I will pay her ten shillings a week which is more than she deserves but I would not like to see her in poverty – where is she?"

Susannah was delighted. She ran into the hallway and called Eliza down from her room. As she came down the stairs Eliza sensed from the look on her mother's face that things were not as bad as they had seemed earlier.

CHAPTER 3

Eliza could hardly contain her excitement as she awaited news from Mr Larchworth concerning the completion of their business. He had various legal papers to draw up and Eliza was called upon several times to sign documents. This was the first time she had had dealings with Solicitors and the experience was to stand her in good stead in years to come.

There was no obligation on Mr Larchworth's part to go to these lengths but he knew from experience that renting property and particularly with so many expensive items of furniture could bring with it many risks. Although he felt he could trust Eliza totally, he also needed to protect his own interests.

When all the legal matters were settled and Eliza had been given the tenancy for not less than six months with the option of extending this by further similar periods, she felt that it was time to inform Mac and her parents of her plans.

She waited until the evening meal was over because mealtimes were always conducted almost entirely in silence. Father might make some observation or other and he might speak quietly to mother but the children were not allowed to speak unless directly requested to do so by their father. The girls helped to clear away and wash the dishes and then mother would take up her knitting as usual. Nothing was ever bought that could be made and the sound of clicking needles was a permanent feature in the house.

Eliza sat on a small chair near to her parents and taking a deep breath, began her explanation.

"Well, father, mother, I have finally found myself a little house to live in. I hope you are pleased for me".

Her parents looked up and stared at her. She had to keep her head lowered in case she might laugh. She was so excited at the prospect of having a house of her own that she wanted nothing to spoil it for her.

"Who on earth has agreed to give you a roof over your head then? Someone who has no concern for his reputation I assume." Father's tone was both derisory and arrogant.

"I sought help from a friend and I am renting a small house at a modest price. It is furnished very tastefully and I can remain there for as long as I wish". Eliza was proud of herself. She was speaking with confidence and resolve and she knew that Mac would have approved.

She went on "I shall be hiring a cart to take my possessions over to the house tomorrow and I shall sleep there tomorrow night for the first time. I am very happy with my decision and I hope you will be happy for me. I shall visit you often and I shall still be at the studio each day".

James and Susannah looked at each other and for once James did not know what to say. He picked up his book and carried on reading. Susannah wanted to know more and she started to ask Eliza all about the house. Where was it? How many rooms? How much was she paying in rent? Eliza was thrilled to talk to her mother in this way. She had longed to do so for weeks but had to be sure that father could not spoil anything. Meanwhile James pretended to read his book, all the while listening intently to the conversation between the two women he loved most in the entire world.

The following day Eliza rose early and began to pack her belongings into several large travelling bags and some boxes. The boy would be arriving with the cart at eleven and she must not keep him waiting. There were things that she needed and things that she wanted. There were things she wanted to leave in her room in her parents' home in order that part of her would always remain there. She hoped that her decision had been the right one. There was no turning back now, however and she would have to learn from her mistakes if indeed she had made any.

She was ready long before she heard the sound of the cart coming along the cobbled street. Their house was on the crest of a hill and the horse slowed down somewhat as it approached the house. The boy came into the house and carried the bags and boxes out to the cart. Susannah hovered around, putting on a brave face now that her daughter had made up her mind to leave and it was actually happening. She consoled herself with the fact that she was not going to be far away and no matter what happened, they would always remain close friends.

When the last of the bags was carefully stowed, the boy asked Eliza if she wanted to ride with him to the house. She saw no reason not to and it would mean that she could open up the house for him when he got there. He helped her up beside him and set off back down the hill. Susannah watched them go with a certain degree of envy. If only she were twenty-one again and could begin life anew. What changes would she have made? Probably none; she loved James and her children and they were the result of her having made the decisions she did when she was sixteen.

Eliza almost jumped down from the cart as they arrived at the house. This was her big moment as she took the key from her bag and put it into the lock. As the door opened, she smelled the faint aroma of tobacco and from the living room stepped Mr Larchworth, arms outstretched to greet her.

"I wanted to be the first to welcome you into your new home" he said smiling broadly. Eliza hugged him and then stopped short. Standing in the doorway behind her was the carter's boy, carrying two of her bags. No doubt he would transmit the details of this little scene to his master and soon the town would be buzzing with yet another scandal regarding the infamous Millard woman.

"Oh, Uncle Thomas, how wonderful of you to come", she cried.

The boy grinned to himself. Did they think he was stupid or something? Uncle indeed!

Thomas and the boy carried the bags and boxes according to Eliza's directions and then the boy left, handsomely tipped by Mr Larchworth.

"I hope he didn't think I was being indiscreet, hugging you like that", she confided in Thomas.

"Oh I am sure he thought nothing of it. You called me 'uncle' in a most convincing manner".
Thomas Larchworth was more than happy with the situation. Eliza lived in his house; he had a key and could visit whenever her pleased and she had certainly hugged him quite spontaneously.

"Well I must leave you to sort out your belongings, are you sure you will be alright by yourself?"

"I am sure I will, thank you Thomas. It will seem strange being alone for a while but I am sure that I will soon have many friends visiting me and I intend to employ a girl to live in and do the housework. So you need not worry, I shall manage quite nicely".

As he walked away from the house, Thomas Larchworth wondered about the friends whom Eliza expected to call. Had he assumed wrongly that Eliza was unattached or did she have a young man who might prove difficult?

Eliza had been right in imagining it would seem strange waking up in an empty house. She opened her eyes and looked around her. At first she thought it was a dream and then slowly she remembered where she was. She lay there for some time, thinking, planning, dreaming. This had been the first night of her new life. Where would it lead? The first thing she must do that day before she went to the studio was to speak to Mac. She was only too conscious of the speed with which news travelled in that town and she was not going to allow him to hear her news from anyone else.

She decided that the best thing to do was go to his surgery. It was only a short walk from there to the studio and she could be there in less than half an hour. Putting on her coat, hat and gloves, she opened her front door and locking it carefully behind her she stepped out from her own home for the first of many days.

When she arrived at the surgery there were already several people waiting to see the doctor. Women with shawls wrapped around their babies and themselves, were huddled by the wall to keep warm. Men in cloth caps and faces blackened by coal dust from the pit were waiting in morose silence. Such sad unhappy people, all trusting that the doctor, Eliza's Mac, would cure their ills and make life a little more bearable for them. Eliza had equal faith in him. He was the only thing that mattered in her life.

She felt guilty, pushing to the front of this pathetic little line of people, but she had to see him as soon as possible. She pushed open the front door and the nurse inside came towards her. She knew Eliza well and wondered what would be the outcome of this strange relationship. Eliza and the doctor had been childhood friends; surely it was not still so innocent."

"Is the doctor alone?" Eliza asked, tentatively.

"He is just about to begin surgery but I will tell him you are here Miss Millard"

The nurse disappeared into Mac's consulting room and almost immediately Eliza heard his voice, the voice she had fallen in love with so many years ago and which still sent a shiver down her spine.

"Go along in, he can spare you a few minutes".

Eliza bustled into the room and closed the door behind her. Her face was flushed and she could barely contain herself. She ran towards him and he took her in his arms. They kissed and then he pulled away from her, still holding her in his arms.

"Oh Eliza, it is wonderful to hold you again. It seems such a long time since we were together. Where have you been?"

"Oh I have so much to tell you and I could not wait any longer. That is why I have come here before going to the studio. I will not keep you any longer because there are people waiting outside who need you even more than I do. Would you meet me from the studio this afternoon and we will walk home together? Then I can tell you the most exciting things that have happened to me".

The day dragged slowly for Eliza. The clients at the studio were more demanding than ever and her father was not in a friendly mood, as she had expected. Aunt Lucy fussed and James was irritated by her. Eliza just longed for the day to end and for Mac to meet her outside the studio. When he finally arrived, Eliza excused herself and pulling on her coat she left the shop hurriedly.

"Now then what is this news you have to tell me?"
"I have left my parents' house".
The young man stopped in his tracks and turned to face Eliza, taking her by the shoulders".

"You have left your parents' house? Eliza, what on earth do you mean?"
"Well life was becoming intolerable there. I had no life of my own, I was questioned about my actions all the time and they thought you were unsuitable for me. Then there are the children. I love them all but I do not intend to be an unpaid nursemaid all my life and that is how I was being treated. I had to help to bring up the younger ones. So I decided

to rent my own house. I did not tell you about it until it was finalised because I wanted you to see how capable I could be". She was quite breathless when she finished.

"And where is this house? Am I allowed to know that?" When he teased her like this she knew he was happy with the situation.

"We are almost there. It is quite near to my parents' house and to the studio and so I do not have too far to walk to visit either place".

They had arrived at Eliza's house and she took out her key to unlock the door and then she stopped. It was unlocked. Mac saw the look of concern on her face.
"What is it?" he asked.
"The door, it is unlocked and I know I locked it this morning". Eliza was worried that he might think she could have been careless enough to leave it unlocked.

Mac opened the door and went in ahead of her. This was not the way Eliza had intended it to be. She wanted to invite him inside and play the hostess to him, but she was afraid there might be an intruder and was glad of his protective action.

Suddenly Eliza sensed that familiar aroma – Mr Larchworth's tobacco! She tried to get into the living room ahead of Mac but he was too quick for her. As he went into the room, Thomas looked up. His face was a picture of incredulity and embarrassment.

"Who the devil are you"? shouted Mac.

Thomas sprang to his feet. " Thomas Larchworth, I am the owner of this property. I just called round to see that everything was in order for Miss Millard's return this evening".

"Then I would be grateful if you did not make a habit of this practice. It is very disconcerting for a young lady to arrive home to find her front door unlocked and a man sitting in her armchair, even if he is the owner of the property". Mac was as ever firm but pleasant in his attitude.

Thomas had not expected this. After Eliza's manner towards him the previous day he had anticipated a warm welcome whenever he was there to greet her; he had obviously misread the situation. This man, whoever he was, was a force to be reckoned with.

After that, Thomas paid fewer visits to Eliza. Mac insisted that if it were necessary for him to visit he should make an appointment and not use his front door key.

Now the two lovers were able to see much more of each other. Mac would call on his way to the surgery in the morning and Eliza would make him a cup of tea. They would sit and drink their tea together and just be happy.

Always their behaviour was discreet as they did not wish to endanger their reputations more than was necessary.

Mac was much sought after to speak at meetings of the Secular Society and to groups of medical practitioners. On these occasions Eliza would accompany him. Soon after Eliza moved into her new home, he invited her to accompany him to such a meeting which was to be held in London. While Eliza was living with her parents it had been impossible for him to ask her to go with him. Now it seemed highly probable.

Eliza was thrilled at the prospect of the train journey to London and seeing sights which she had merely heard of previously. She also realised for the first time that she could make her own decisions. She did not need to consult her parents. Mac, however regarded the occasion as one during which he might prove his love for Eliza in a much more intimate way than he had been able to do up to now.

He wrote to the Hotel he often used when in London, reserving a double room on this occasion. Since many of the other participants at such functions were as unorthodox in their views as he was, he felt sure that few eyebrows would be raised.

Eliza agreed because she was happy for the world to see them together as man and wife which is how they would appear once they were away from their home town. They talked the matter over and decided to embark on this great adventure.

When the day of the journey arrived, they were as happy as any newly married couple setting off on their honeymoon. Although Eliza had not had a wedding dress and there was no church ceremony or marriage certificate, this was the day on which they were to give themselves to each other for ever. During the long train journey they laughed and held hands and when no one could see, Mac would kiss Eliza fondly. She was happier than she had imagined was possible.

When they arrived at the hotel they were shown to their room. It was a splendid room with heavy curtains draped around the bed. There were silk covered armchairs and settees and a table upon which stood a huge bowl of pink roses. Mac took Eliza over to the table and pointed to the gold embossed card nestling among the flowers. Eliza took the card in her hand and read "Love me, love me and forever!"
Eliza turned and kissed him. A clock somewhere struck five and Eliza knew that five o'clock in the afternoon would always be a special time of day for her. He helped her off with her coat and then stood before her, passion rising within him. Slowly he steered her towards the bed and gently lowered her onto it. This, she knew was the moment she had wondered about for so long and now that it had arrived it seemed quite natural. She did not feel inadequate or inexperienced. It was as if she had an inner instinct leading her on, showing here how every move should be made.

As Mac began to remove her clothes she helped him without making it too obvious that she was doing so. Women's clothes often bore complicated fastenings and men were sometimes unfamiliar with these. Mac did not seem in the least troubled and it occurred to Eliza that he had probably seen many women undressing in his consulting room. Mac gazed down on Eliza's nakedness. He too had waited so long for this moment and now he intended to savour it. He refused to take his eyes from her as he began to remove his own clothes. Eliza took sensuous delight from being adored in this fashion. She watched Mac's gaze shift from her face and travel slowly along the length of her body, stopping to take in the sheer exquisite beauty of her figure. He reached out to touch her flawless skin and Eliza shivered in ecstasy at the touch of his fingers on her breasts. Slowly with the softest of touches, the surgeon's hands explored every inch of her body, touching parts which made Eliza cry out in delight.

This was love-making at his most intense and passionate and it continued until their passions were sated.

Afterwards they lay entwined together until they fell asleep.

Suddenly Mac awoke with a start.

'Oh no! it is almost seven-thirty and I am due to speak at the first meeting at eight o'clock."

Eliza leapt from the bed and putting on a robe, began to gather together the clothes which had lain scattered from their lovemaking.

"I had hoped to be with you, but as you are late perhaps it would be better if I stayed here this evening".

"I will arrange for some supper to be served here in our room if you like. I will eat out after the meeting."

He washed and dressed hurriedly, kissed her and was gone.

She felt that in a few brief hours she had gone from the heights to the depths. She began to unpack their bags and as she did so she realised that she was seeing parts of him she had known nothing of before. She put his underclothes into a drawer and thought how strange it was that she had held his naked body in her arms but had never seen his underwear. She giggled at this. Then she thought of all the other men she knew, men like Thomas Larchworth and the clients at the studio and she wondered whether they wore undergarments such as Mac's and whether they might excite her as much with their bodies as Mac had done. The very thought of Thomas Larchworth's naked body made her feel slightly sick!

From that day they were never to be parted. During those few days in London they loved each other with a passion that neither of them had ever dreamed possible. Each day Mac would leave for the meeting rooms and Eliza sometimes accompanied him, sitting in solitude at the back of the hall and listening to him speaking. When he was not called upon to speak he would sit with Eliza and point out to her the distinguished people assembled there. On one occasion he gave her some money and suggested she might like to visit the excellent shops in London and buy herself some new clothes. She enjoyed this immensely, although she could not wait to return to show him the things she had bought.

The nights however were for them alone. Nights they wished might never end as they lay in each other's arms and each experienced such pleasure that they would remember for the rest of their lives.

Their love grew daily and they knew that there would never be anyone else for either of them. The times when they were apart were agony for them both.

When they returned home, however, life had to resume its normal pattern. Eliza worked hard to make her career and her father's business successful. Mac continued to build up his practice and became one of the most respected doctors in the town.

Eliza worried that she might be in danger of becoming pregnant. This worry was not for herself or for Mac, but again for her family. While she felt that the two of them could live with the stigma attached to their own situation, she could not envisage either of them wishing to inflict the stigma of illegitimacy upon an innocent child.

One evening as they sat after dinner in Eliza's house, she decided to broach the subject.

'Have you ever considered what would happen if we had a baby?"
"A baby, Eliza, why should we have a baby?" it was as if he had never even considered the possibility.

"We might do. These things happen. I worry so much about it because I do not think it would be fair to inflict those sort of problems upon a child".

"I would never dream of allowing such a thing to happen, Eliza, do you not trust me?"

Eliza felt ashamed that she had worried about the matter as it almost seemed to indicate her lack of confidence in him.

Mac sat for some time, apparently deep in thought and then he spoke.

"Actually, I have given the matter some thought. I do not think that we should run the risk of bringing a child into a world such as this. As you say, we can bear the slings and arrows but should we expect a child to do the same. Even if we were living together permanently, a child would be forced into an intolerable situation".
"I am so glad I spoke to you about this," she said "as they say, a trouble shared is a trouble halved."
"You were absolutely right to discuss your fears with me but as a matter of fact, I had already decided what we will do about it"

Eliza was astounded. So he had already decided but had said nothing to her. Did he not consider that the matter concerned her at all? However she said nothing of this. She lived under his spell and would always accept whatever he said.

"I have been aware for some time that you become quite unwell at certain times each month."
Eliza was embarrassed by this. From the time when she first began her monthly periods she had always had one very bad day. Her mother had told her that this was quite a natural thing to happen and that it would be much better when she had had her first child. The remedy was to retire to bed for one day each month, drinking only milk for that day. Not only did this help the pain but also helped the figure.

So Mac had noticed. Well he was a doctor and she supposed he was bound to notice things like that.
"Yes I do get a lot of pain each month and I find that lying in bed helps."
"I would like to take you to see a friend of mine; he is a Gynaecologist, dealing in women's problems. He works in one of the big London hospitals and I am sure he could help you with your problem as well as ensuring that you do not become pregnant."
"What can he do about it?" asked Eliza.
"There have been many improvements made recently in surgical procedures to relieve conditions such as yours. Even women with severe tumours are being helped."
"What do you mean?" Eliza felt a surge of panic running through her body.
"There is an operation to remove the womb. Sometimes the ovaries are removed as well but that would be a little drastic in your case. I am sure that my friend could reassure you about the whole procedure. As a matter of fact I have already made an appointment for you to see him when we go to London next month to the Conference."
It seemed to Eliza that he regarded this as simple an operation as pulling a tooth, but to Eliza it seemed like a sentence of death.
"Is it a dangerous operation?" she asked fearfully.

Mac laughed. She hated it when he did this. She felt like she had done as a small child when she had asked if a toad was a daddy frog. He had laughed at her then and she had felt small and ignorant in comparison with him. Now she felt so again.

"Would I put you in any danger, Eliza?" he asked. "I love you too much. No, my friend is the finest surgeon of his kind. He has performed several of these operations, although they are relatively new and I have every confidence in him. It is becoming clear that disturbances such as yours can also lead to other things. It seems to be the cause of most of the strange behaviour sometimes attributed to women, although I am unwilling to accept some of those theories just yet. Women ought not to be forced to suffer the way they do. If men had to go through this sort of thing every month, I am sure it would have been the focus of much more research."

The matter seemed to be closed as far as Mac was concerned. Eliza on the other hand continued to worry but now that worry was for her own future rather than that of a possible child.

On their next visit to London, the friend was contacted and they went along to see him in his consulting rooms.

He was as gentle in his manner as Mac. Concerned that women had for too long been seen as child-bearing machines, he was anxious that his research and pioneering operations should be put to good use in giving women a better quality of life and the choice of whether they wished to have children or not.

A nurse helped Eliza to undress and she lay down on the couch while the doctor examined her. Only Mac had ever touched in this way before and now she was allowing another man to do so with him sitting across the room. However, this touching gave Eliza a different feeling. She felt a searing pain as his fingers were forced up inside her body. He pressed down hard on her abdomen, pushing her womb down towards his fingers. She clenched her teeth and closed her eyes tightly against the pain. How could Mac have put her through all this?

At last the examination was over and she was told to get dressed. When she returned, the two doctors were deep in conversation. It had been decided that Eliza did indeed require surgery to rectify certain abnormalities in her womb.

Eliza had many questions to ask and they were answered in the most reassuring manner possible.

It would not be a painful operation.
It would not endanger her life.
It would prevent her becoming pregnant.

Eliza and Mac left the hospital after making the necessary arrangements for her operation which would take place here in London the following week.
She decided that she would not tell her family the true nature of the surgery since this might cause them some distress. She would invent some fictional problem requiring surgery instead.

Eliza would speak with her mother as soon as they arrived home. She felt sure that a woman who had borne eleven children would be able to sympathise with her.

As they made the long train journey home, Eliza was silent. She was contemplating the future which lay ahead of her and wondering yet again whether or not she had made the right decision.

Susannah was in the kitchen, supervising the preparation of the evening meal. Eliza kissed her lightly on the cheek and asked her to come and sit down to talk.

'I have to go into hospital, Mother.' Eliza said as casually as she could.
'What on earth for, Eliza? I didn't realise you were unwell. Why did you never confide in me before?' her mother was genuinely distressed about anything which might affect any of her children.

'Well, I didn't want to worry you mother, and there isn't really anything wrong. It is just that one day I would like to have children and it seems at present that I am unlikely to do so unless I have this small operation to put things right. It is nothing serious.'

'Children, Eliza? But you are not even married and nor do you intend to be'

The prospect of an illegitimate child was obviously as distasteful to Susannah as Eliza had expected it to be. She had been right to fear the consequences of becoming pregnant.

'Well having children might change things, you never know' Eliza hoped this might appease her mother - at least for the time being. Susannah, however just stared ahead of her into the fire. Her eldest daughter, her first-born child, the beginning of her own happiness was now heaping coals of fire upon her. Would it never end?

Eliza was terrified of the forthcoming operation. Queen Victoria had had this new anaesthetic for the births of her children and so it was considered safe enough now. However, that was not all that terrified Eliza. Nobody had said so directly but she believed it would mean the end of her chances of ever becoming a mother, her usefulness as a woman would be over and she was still only twenty-six years old.

Before the date which had been fixed for her to enter the hospital, Eliza had to inform Thomas Larchworth that she might be away for a few weeks. She still had little idea of what the operation would entail and she did not know how long it would be before she was able to look after herself once more. The young girl whom she had employed to work for her in the house would not be able to attend to her if she were incapacitated for long. She decided to pay the girl to keep the house in order during her absence but told Mr Larchworth that she was unsure of how long that would be. He was concerned about her health but sensed that this was one of those operations about which women preferred not to be questioned.

She set about purchasing new nightgowns and dressing robes ready for her stay in hospital. She intended always to look her best for Mac.

Then she asked her father to take her photograph. He had done so many times before but this was the first time it had been at her own request. Her father sensed her anxiety and asked her to be truthful about her illness.

'I have no illness father," she said, "I just have to have something done regarding my being able to bear children". She tried to word her reply in such a way that she would not be telling an outright lie. She found it hard to look her father in the face.

James was the father of eleven children but knew little about the workings of women's bodies. He had never been present at a birth and the matter of women's reproductive systems was never discussed. He was positively embarrassed at having to discuss it with his daughter.

"Well, perhaps you will be better afterwards" he said, hoping that once that was sorted out she might come to her senses and start living life as a normal married woman. He wanted the conversation to end and so he gave Eliza a hug and got on with the job of taking her picture.

Eliza had dressed carefully for the portrait. She wore a dress of heavy pale blue calico. Her hair was arranged in braids and curls around the back of her head. The picture was taken from behind with her looking back over her left shoulder at the camera. She had planned it very meticulously as being symbolic of her looking back upon her life. Several years later she sent a copy of the picture to her brother Eddie and on the back she wrote:
Seven and twenty now – a great age when youth has lost its self-consciousness and grown a little sobered by experience'

When Mac took Eliza into hospital, she was impressed by the obvious high regard in which he was held by all the staff there. Doctors and nurses alike shook him by the hand and wished Eliza a speedy recovery. What she did not realise at the time was just how rare this operation actually was. Neither she nor the surgeons who were to perform it truly understood its implications.

The operation was performed as planned but Eliza found it difficult to make as speedy a recovery as she had hoped. She had never anticipated the amount of blood she would continue to lose. Mac was obviously concerned but no man on earth could ever understand how she really felt. As she lay in the tiny hospital bed, tearfulness overcame her again and again. She really could not imagine why she had agreed to the operation in the first place but she would never dispute any decision made by her wonderful doctor.

Each day the surgeon came to see her and comforted her when she was tearful. He reassured her that the operation had been a resounding success but told her that she would need complete rest for about six months if she was to recover fully.
Six months!! She had told her parents it was a simple operation!!

When Mac came to see her she told him what the surgeon had said.

"Well that means we can spend more time together. You will not be able to go to the studio for a long time so I can spend all my spare time with you. As your doctor I would need to take special care of you. We will employ a nurse for you as well. How does that sound?"

Mac never ceased to astound Eliza. That was probably one of the reasons why she was fascinated by him. Nothing was ever a problem to him. He had the whole matter sorted out in less time than it took some people to choose a chocolate from a box.

And that was how it was. He decided everything and then told Eliza. Why, she wondered did he never discuss anything with her? Did he think that because he was older than she, he must take charge of everything? If they were a real married couple, surely he would not behave in this way.

Eliza looked at him with adoration in her eyes. "Are you ever going to say that we are going to live together permanently?"

Mac looked uneasy. He turned away from her and began to stride across the ward. Then quite suddenly he turned back and came right up to her. He sat on the edge of the bed and held her close.

"Eliza I do not think I could ever let you go again. I have fought against the desire to take you away because I know that the time is not right yet. However strong our feelings are for each other, I feel we still must consider our parents and their views"

How typical this was of him. Always mindful of others.

When the day eventually arrived when she was able to leave the hospital, a horse drawn ambulance collected her and took her directly to the station. She was transferred to a wheelchair and wheeled carefully to the door of a first class compartment. Inside, everything had been made ready for her to enjoy as comfortable a journey as possible in the circumstances.

Her mother had tried to insist that she went back home but Mac had instructed the surgeon to inform all enquirers that she needed peace and quiet. A house full of children was certainly not conducive to that.

On leaving the train she was again transferred to an ambulance and the short journey to her home began.

The ambulance drew up outside the house and Eliza was carried into a wheelchair and thence up the steps into the little house. Had she not been so weak and ill, she would have jumped for joy at the sight of her house which she had missed so much. Mac had arranged for a couch to be placed in the window so that she could see out and so that she need not be negotiating the stairs just yet. She was placed gently on the couch and her pillows arranged for her greatest comfort. The rugs were placed over her and it was only then that she saw Thomas Larchworth standing in the doorway. He was carrying a basket of flowers. Coming over to her he looked down and said softly "I have missed you Eliza."

Eliza glanced to where Mac was standing. His face was set with a look of utter disapproval.

"Thank you Thomas," she said, trying to ignore Mac. "It is gratifying to see that you have looked after the house so well for me in my absence" Catriona the maid looked on shyly and Thomas brought her forward.
"This is the young lady you must thank, Eliza she is the one who has worked hard to have everything just right for your return."
"Isn't it wonderful, doctor, to know that the house has been cared for so well in my absence?"
Eliza felt that she had handled the situation admirably. Now no one felt threatened and everybody knew where they stood.

Had she not felt so unwell, she might have censured Mac for his attitude but as it was she felt the matter should end there.

Eliza reached up with her hand to touch Mac's as it rested on the back of the couch.

He stood silently as Thomas Larchworth left the house and Catriona disappeared into the kitchen. He did not respond to Eliza's touch. This was the first time he had ever experienced jealousy. He had always had his own way; no one had challenged him in what he decided to do or to have. This time he was being challenged. Although he admired the sensitive way in which Eliza had dealt with Larchworth, he knew that the matter was certainly not at an end.

"Do you think you will soon recover, now that you are in your own home?" Mac finally asked.

"Oh, if only," she gasped, "if only you could stay here with me. Then I am sure I would soon be well again."

"You need time to yourself, so that you can get stronger and also there is a lot of healing to be done by your body" Mac was finding it difficult to deal with emotions which were quite alien to him.

Eliza was stunned.

She had at least expected some sort of agreement from him.

The door opened and Catriona entered.

She was several years younger than Catriona and very pretty. She carried the bag which Eliza had brought with her from the hospital.

"Would madam like to retire now?"

Mac decided that this was the moment when he should leave.

Placing a kiss on her cheek, he bade her goodnight and hurried out through the door.

Eliza's heart thumped at the realisation that he had gone. He had left in an apparent hurry. Here she was, home after weeks in hospital and he had just left. What was troubling him? Again, however, she said nothing. She nodded to the maid who assumed that Eliza was so ill that she had not the strength to answer.

With Catriona's help, Eliza prepared herself for bed. Her long hair was brushed until it shone and the nightgown she chose certainly set off the glow of her skin. Painfully she climbed into bed and realised that it was still only late afternoon. As the clock struck five she was transported back to that day in London when they had first scaled the heights of passion together. Her body still throbbed with the pain of the operation and she could scarcely imagine ever experiencing such emotions again.

"The nurse will be coming to see you soon and she will decide what you should eat" Catriona gathered together Eliza's clothes and made to leave the room.

"Catriona," Eliza called after her.
"Yes ma'am"
"Have you any family, brothers, sisters, parents I mean?"

"Well, you see Ma'am, my parents are both dead. I try to earn what I can to support my younger brothers and sisters. They live with my aunt" The tears began to flow as Eliza began to wonder if she had been selfish in leaving her parents rather than helping to support her younger brothers and sisters.

"There, there" comforted Catriona. "You must not upset yourself over my problems. Just concentrate on getting well."

There was a knock at the door and Catriona admitted a woman whom they both took to be the nurse. She was efficient but unfriendly. Eliza did not think she was going to like this woman at all.
"Now girl" she spoke sharply to Catriona. "We will have some soup and then some fresh vegetables with a little boiled fish"
Catriona dashed off to do her bidding and Eliza looked on, decidedly disconcerted. She decided she must ask a few questions.
"I hope you won't think it rude of me to ask these questions, but who exactly employed you?"
"Doctor MacLoghlin ma'am," she replied tersely.
"And just how long have you known the doctor?"
"As long as I have been working at the hospital. He is such a dedicated man and we all have a great deal of respect for him. I was quite flattered when he asked me to come here to work for him".

"Shall we make certain of our facts, nurse?" Eliza insisted. "While you are in my house, you will be working for me and not the doctor."

The nurse was taken aback by this and Eliza felt quite proud of herself. Eliza was not sure what she had expected to happen next, but whatever it had been, she certainly was surprised by what did happen.

The nurse suddenly fell to the floor, sobbing uncontrollably. She knelt by Eliza's bed and seized her by the hands.

"Please do not tell the doctor that you are displeased with me" she pleaded.

"Nurse, how could I do that? You have done nothing to displease me. I am merely letting you know that I am your employer and not the doctor, so that you know whose instructions you should follow". Eliza was devastated at the pitiful sight before her.

"I am sure we are both going to be very pleased with your work. Please dry your eyes and get on with what you have to do. I am sure you would not wish the doctor to return and see you in this state"

Eliza lay back on her pillows. The tears with which she was becoming so familiar returned.

After that the nurse was attentive and silent. Catriona brought in the meal and Eliza asked the nurse if she would stay and share it with her. Eliza could not face the prospect of being alone. However, the nurse had to leave and Catriona had other work to do so Eliza lay there and wished for the noisy voices of her brothers and sisters. She even wished her father would come to see her, although she was sure that if he did so, they would be disagreeing before too long.

As it was, nobody came to see her. She lay there as the room grew darker and only the flickering firelight lit the room. How long would she have to stay her alone, she wondered. She was beginning to realise that she might have to spend many hours here alone.

Just as the waterfall that she felt had replaced her eyes began to burst its banks yet again, drenching her cheeks, the door opened and there stood Mac. He was carrying a tray containing two glasses of wine. He closed the door with his foot and walked over to the bed. He placed the tray down on the bedside table and bent to kiss Eliza. Then he lit the lamps before settling down on the chair by the bed.

"Wine, madam?" he asked with a smile.

"Yes thank you, kind sir" Eliza replied and all doubts faded from her mind.

"This is very peaceful" she managed to say at last.
"That is exactly how I hoped you would feel" he said, pouring another glass of wine for himself. "All you need worry about now is getting stronger so that you can leave this room and get out into the sunshine".

Eliza sat gazing ahead of her. The room was warm and friendly but there were so many things she wanted to ask. She wanted to know about the nurse he had employed to take care of her. Why was she so afraid of Mac? She dared not ask the questions however, because somehow she feared the answers.

Mac looked towards her and saw the tears once more welling over her eyelids.

"Oh dear, Eliza, please do not cry. Women do sometimes do feel a little tearful after this operation. It is because you are weak and have lost a lot of blood. It is probably also because you feel a little sorry for yourself."
"Yes, I do feel a little that way. I wonder whether I should indeed have gone through with this whole thing".

"Of course you should" Mac insisted. "There would be no point in bringing children into such a world as this. We are responsible people. If more people did this then the world would be a better place. I know we have done the right thing".

Eliza felt a pang at his use of the word 'We'. She was the one lying in this bed and the one who would never be able to bear children. She had believed that the main purpose of the operation had been to relieve her of her monthly suffering, but now she realised that there was more to it than that. It had been an excuse. The true reason had been to prevent her from having children, to conform to Mac's beliefs.

She wondered whether Mac could possibly understand what that meant to her. She had watched her poor mother bowed down with constant childbearing and had vowed never to suffer so herself. But never to have any children at all, that was not how she had intended it to be. It was too late now, however. She had been guided, rightly or wrongly and she could only allow herself to be sure she had done the right thing.

The clock in the hall struck seven and Mac took his watch from his pocket. "I have patients to attend now, my dear; Catriona will be in to see to you later. I doubt if I will be back before you have supper, so I will say 'Good night' to you now."

He kissed her briefly but tenderly and left the room before she had time to reply.

The feelings which overwhelmed her at that moment were confused and frightening. She had sacrificed everything for this man, her natural function as a woman, her family and her home. All he could do was leave her in the care of a servant. She felt totally bereft and abandoned.

When Catriona came in to remove the glasses and tray she thought Eliza was asleep. Creeping quietly over to the bed, she was startled when

Eliza suddenly said "Would you like to have a baby, Catriona?" The young girl was speechless. "Well, would you?" Eliza repeated, becoming quite agitated.

"I expect I would, one day, Ma'am, but not yet. I haven't even got a young man at present." Catriona blushed and Eliza was sorry for the way she had spoken to her.

"I will never be able to have children now you see, since the operation. They took everything out of me that I could have a baby with" Now that Eliza was hearing herself say the words she felt she must go on. "I was ill you see and the doctor arranged everything. He is so kind, so thoughtful. I really have to be very grateful to him".

Catriona stood by the bed, holding the tray of tea things. She wondered whether she should leave the room or stay. How like the doctor it was to take care of the lady in this way – and he so busy as well. She waited until she was quite sure that Eliza had finished speaking before she turned to leave.

"Will you come back to sit with me when you have finished your jobs?" Eliza said in a pitiful voice.

"Of course I will ma'am" she replied, although she did not think she was going to enjoy the experience.

It was nearly nine o'clock when Catriona returned to Eliza's room. She was carrying a supper tray. She set it down by the bed and helped Eliza to sit up, arranging her pillows so as to support her. It reminded Eliza of the time she had been ill in bed as a child and her mother arranged her pillows like that. Her mother called it 'making an armchair' when she fluffed up the pillows and surrounded her with them. The thought of her mother at home, no doubt suffering the anguish of not knowing how Eliza was, filled her with sorrow.

"Tomorrow I would like you to take a message to my parents" she said.
"Certainly, ma'am. Do they live far away?"

"No, but they do not know that I have left the hospital. I am sure my mother would come to see me if she knew. I feel so weak; I don't think I could even write a letter at the moment. Do you think you could write it for me if I told you what to write?"

Catriona's heart sank. Cook, clean, sew, run errands, do anything else for the lady, but write or read!!!

"I am afraid I cannot write well enough for that Ma'am" she confessed.

"Well my writing is pretty dreadful I must admit, so I don't suppose it is going to be any worse for my being ill. Never mind, I shall manage somehow."

Eliza hoped that she had passed over Catriona's admission without too much embarrassment.

After she had eaten her light supper, Eliza talked for a while to Catriona about her home and her family and then, feeling tired, lay back on the pillows.

"I think I will try to sleep now Catriona, will you please turn out the lights and in the morning will you bring me some paper and a pen and ink so that I might write my letter?"

"Yes Ma'am, good night"

Turning out the lamps, Catriona quietly left the room. Eliza lay awake in the darkness for some time. She wondered where he was now. She imagined she heard him open the front door and come in to bid her 'good night'. No one did come however and she fell into a deep sleep. Some hours later she awoke with a start, wondering where she was. Something had woken her but now she did not know what it was. Somewhere in another part of the house she thought she heard laughter, but sleep overcame her once more before she could give more thought to the matter.

The morning sun through the window fell on to Eliza's face and she awoke. She turned over in bed and had some difficulty in orientating herself. The pain in her abdomen reminded her of why she was there. Then she felt a sticky dampness beneath her and realised with horror that she must be bleeding heavily. There was a small bell on the bedside table and she leaned over to grasp it. The pain as she did so was excruciating and seemed to cause the bleeding to become heavier than ever. The sound of the bell seemed abnormally loud in the still silent house and almost at once the door opened to her left. Catriona stood there in her dressing gown, an anxious look on her face.

"What is it Ma'am?"

"Oh I am so sorry; I did not intend to disturb you at such an early hour. I seem to be bleeding rather heavily; can you help me?" Eliza was mortified at having to make such a request of the girl, but she was desperate.

Catriona had never had to do anything like this for another woman and she felt embarrassed at having to do so now. However, between the two of them they soon had Eliza clean and comfortable once more. They both returned to bed.

The clock in the hall struck six and somewhere, not far away, Eliza heard the door open and then close. She heard the sounds of footsteps as Catriona set about her tasks of lighting the fire and then silence returned. She could sleep no more. She craved companionship more than anything else and her worries as to where her beloved Mac could be eclipsed all other thoughts from her mind.

Then quite suddenly the house seemed to come to life. Catriona could be heard sweeping and there was the unmistakable aroma of breakfast being cooked. The door opened and Catriona appeared with morning tea. She also carried in her apron pocket some writing paper and envelopes.

"I will bring the pen and ink later, Ma'am. I couldn't carry it with the tray."

"Oh, thank you, I am so glad you remembered." Eliza was grateful for even the smallest kindness, so depressed was she feeling emotionally.

"Oh and the doctor said he will be in to see you as soon as he gets back from his rounds." Catriona busied herself, straightening the bedclothes, while Eliza sipped her tea.

"When did he say that?" Eliza could not imagine how Catriona had received such a message.

"He called on his way to surgery, but you were sound asleep"

Eliza tried to hide her disappointment. She imagined him coming in to have breakfast with her, reading his morning paper in her room just as he had done so often in those months before she went into hospital.

"I think he had to go to the hospital to see a patient he admitted late last night." Catriona spoke in an assured knowledgeable manner about it.

"I see," murmured Eliza, "had he eaten breakfast?"

"Oh yes, I cooked it for him when he called. He was really disappointed not to be able to speak to you but he told me to let you sleep""

Eliza was much happier now. She must have slept much more soundly than she had realised. She was filled with far fewer doubts and concerns. Catriona collected the tea things and made to leave the room.

"What time does the nurse arrive?" asked Eliza at last.

"She should stay here all the time. She has a bed here in the house." Catriona explained.

Eliza realised that Mac must have made all these arrangements without her knowledge. She also realised that her comments to the nurse must have confused the poor woman beyond all reason.

"I wonder why she has not been to see me before this" said Eliza, looking up at Catriona with her big tearful eyes. "I am in some discomfort and I would like her to come as soon as possible".

Catriona smiled and left the room.

Eliza felt as though she was living through some sort of nightmare. She had come here expecting to be cared for and nursed gently back to health and was beginning to believe that she would have had far more attention from her mother at home, regardless of the children milling around the place.

The door opened and the nurse appeared. Now that Eliza had the opportunity to see her in daylight she realised that she was quite young, attractive and really very kind. Eliza was sorry she had treated her cruelly.

"Now my dear, I believe we have a little problem," she said softly to Eliza.

"Yes, nurse, we have."

Eliza could not avoid the hint of sarcasm in her reply. Mac always included himself in Eliza's problems, now the nurse was doing the same.

"We are very uncomfortable in this bed, it is damp with blood and we need a change of bed linen and dressings".

Eliza felt quite self-satisfied to be speaking to the nurse in this way.

"There is no need for that is there?" chastised the nurse."We'll soon have you comfortable again."

The nurse passed into the kitchen and returned with an efficiently laid trolley. It contained all the things she would need to look after Eliza. She examined her carefully and seemed pleased with what she saw. Eliza tried to squint down to see for herself but received a sharp reminder that she should keep still. She was beginning to think that this was not her own body at all but one she was looking after for someone else. How she wished that were really the case. She would willingly give this one back to his rightful owner and take her own in exchange. Warm water, heated on the kitchen fire, was brought to bathe her and she was soon feeling much more comfortable.

"I would like to help you to get out of bed while we change the sheets" said the nurse. Since Eliza could not do this by herself, Catriona came in to help and the two women got Eliza to her feet and then into a chair. As she stood up, albeit for a second, she felt the blood flooding from her. Panic seized her and she flung herself into the chair.

"Oh help me, please help me" she screamed to nobody in particular. As the red stain grew larger and deeper over the front of her nightgown, the nurse realised that something was sadly wrong.

""Catriona!" ordered the nurse, "get the doctor!"
It seemed that Mac appeared at the door almost immediately, but Eliza was in no state to question how this was.
He was followed closely by another man whom Eliza had seen at meetings she had attended with Mac.
"This is Doctor Shepherd. There are certain ethics regarding doctors treating their own families. Since you are my family, I have asked Doctor Shepherd to attend you."

He examined Eliza gently and compassionately and spoke with calming words. He was not unduly worried about the haemorrhaging and explained to the nurse and to Eliza that this was quite normal in the circumstances. It might continue for several days but would eventually stop. The main problem was how to contain the flow. She would need to have her dressings changed frequently and the nurse was instructed to attend to this every hour. She also needed to remain flat in bed with her feet raised slightly.

Mac meanwhile had been pondering something to himself.

"How long is it since you looked at the patient, Nurse?"he asked.
"I have tended her constantly throughout the night, doctor" she lied.
Eliza looked at Mac and he knew the look well enough to know that this was not true.
"How many times have you changed the dressings?" he asked.
"As often as was necessary, doctor".
"Where did you dispose of the soiled ones?" he continued his questioning.
"In the kitchen grate, "she said. Her eyes were becoming more and more averted as his questions began to frighten her.

"I see" he pondered, ", so the fire is kept burning all night, is that so? Catriona, did you tend the fire throughout the night?"
"No sir, I lit it this morning" she feared both the doctor and the nurse, but she knew that it was still better for her to tell the truth.
"So nurse, where did you dispose of the dressings during the night?" Mac was becoming irritated by these quite blatant lies.

Eliza decided she had to intervene. She merely wanted them all to go and leave her alone with Mac, so she spoke up.
"I was so tired last night that I asked the nurse to leave me alone during the night and then I realised this morning that I had been wrong to leave it for such a long time"

"I need to be able to trust both you Nurse and you, Catriona to look after Miss Millard at all times." He seemed to be choosing the next words very carefully. After a pause he continued "...even if she does tell you to leave her alone"

A smile played around his lips and he cast a look in Eliza's direction, which she knew meant he fully understood what Eliza had been trying to do.

From that time Eliza had the best of attention. It had not been evident at first that Eliza was any more than another patient of the doctor's. However as time went by it became obvious that she was very much more than that. The nurse had seen many patients come and go but none whom the doctor cared for like this one.

Now that he had seen fit to engage a second doctor it was obvious what kind of relationship theirs was.

The rest of the day passed much as the previous one had done. Catriona and the nurse came and went and Eliza was cosseted and cared for but Mac never appeared again.

While she was alone, Eliza started to write the letter she had planned.
"Dear Mother and Father
I wanted you to know that I am now out of hospital and back in my own home to convalesce. The house is very peaceful and there are people to care for me every hour of the day and night. I miss you all very much, dear parents, and I think of my beloved brothers and sisters constantly. The doctor cares for his patients most of the time and I fear he has not enough time to spend with me, but he has made sure that I have the very best of attention during his absence.
Think of me.
Your affectionate daughter,
Eliza".

The letter was placed in the envelope and carefully sealed and it awaited delivery to her parents' home. She hoped she had not hinted in the letter that she was desperately unhappy. Her parents had never wanted her to come here in the first place and would seize upon the first opportunity to insist on her returning home. At the moment she would gladly have welcomed such insistence but she had to look to the future, her future with Mac. When she was fully recovered they would begin the life they had planned together.

The days and weeks dragged by with increasing tedium. Eliza began to regain her strength and now she was able to leave her bed for longer and longer periods of time. The nurse was pleased with her progress and Mac spent some part of each day talking with her and telling her about his days.

She noticed however that he seemed to tire easily. The many meetings he used to attend grew fewer and fewer and he seemed content to sit for longer at her bedside without having to rush away to some important engagement.

On one occasion, Eliza caught him unawares, holding his head in his hands and appearing to be in great pain.

"What on earth is the matter?" she took his hand and it felt hat and clammy.

"Oh it is nothing. A little headache, that is all. Too much work and not enough sleep I expect."

But Eliza was concerned. He had never been physically strong but he had never allowed anything to come between him and his work. Now he looked like a man who was completely exhausted.

As Eliza's strength grew, so Mac's seemed to diminish. The time came when she felt well enough to visit her father's studio once more. Mac accompanied her. As they walked down the familiar street together, people stared and it was obvious what they were thinking. 'That Millard woman has been up to her old tricks again' Rumours began to circulate about the operation she had recently recovered from. Most of the gossip centred on it having been an abortion. Such events were not uncommon amongst the very women who were now gossiping. They all knew someone in a back street who would get rid of their unwanted burdens for the price of a pint of ale. Many died from the results of such butchery. The richer classes of course were able to pay for qualified surgeons to perform the abortions secretly at a vast price. So where did Eliza stand. Had she been to a back street abortionist or had her rich doctor friend paid an enormous price?

The truth was beyond the comprehension of most of the local women. In fact it was only by asking a lot of questions that Eliza had discovered that such operations were indeed very rare. This was why she had needed to go to London for the best surgical techniques available. In fact, only for the last twenty years had it been considered safe enough to perform it at all except in the case of the severest tumours. Before that, the expectation of life after a Hysterectomy, as she had discovered the procedure was called, was never longer than a year and that only in the rarest cases. Had Eliza known this from the outset, she was sure she would never have agreed to the operation. However, she had survived because of the care of her wonderful Doctor Mac.

Once she heard about the current rumours, she decided there was only one thing to do.

That evening, she called Catriona to her and spoke frankly about the way people were gossiping. She wondered whether Catriona herself knew what the operation had been.

"Well Ma'am, I know it was something to do with having babies. I expect something went wrong that is how I looked at it"

"Oh, dear Catriona. Nothing went wrong, everything went right. I had something wrong with me which meant that I could not have children, so the surgeon removed my womb. Because this is quite a rare operation, most people have never heard of it. They seem to have got the idea that I have had an abortion or something. This is just not true. If you hear anyone talking about it, would you please put them right? They are more likely to talk in front of you than me".

Catriona promised she would give anyone a piece of her mind who dared to say such bad things about her mistress.

Although she could not be certain of it, Eliza felt that after this, people did seem to look at her in a slightly less accusatory way.

That evening Mac said he needed to discuss something very important with Eliza and so Catriona was given the night off.

"Look Eliza, please be patient while I try to explain this to you. Over the past few years there have been many advances made in medicine and surgery. A colleague and I have been working very hard on many new developments. Sometimes they have been successful, sometimes they have not. Many of our patients were terminally ill when they came to us and an operation was their only chance of survival. After the operations they needed careful nursing and we felt they needed somewhere other than hospital in which to recover. Together we bought a large house in Southport where we could look after them. If they made a recovery, they went home and paid us a large sum of money because they were so grateful to us for saving their lives. If they died, we saw to the arrangements and nobody was hurt"

Eliza listened with interest to all this, all the while marvelling that he had never thought fit to discuss it with her before.

"My colleague is no longer with me and it is going to mean I shall have to spend more time over there at the house"

"So why is he no longer with you? "

"We had a violent disagreement; over you actually"

"Over me!" Eliza felt she was reading this in some book of fiction.

"Yes, he thought that my love for you was detrimental to my career and my work. He wanted me to devote my life to him and our work rather than to you."

"I see". Eliza was silent for some time. She had heard somewhere that there were some men who loved other men rather than women. Could this be what Mac was now meaning?

"Did he love you?" Eliza asked tentatively, half dreading that he would confirm her worst fears and yet not wanting him to think her stupid for even considering such a possibility.

"I think he did, yes, but such matters are not for you to concern yourself with. I love you. He was a valued colleague and friend, that is all you need to believe" "but where did he go?" Eliza was not going to let the matter drop so easily.

"He died" Mac turned and walked away towards the window. He seemed to be lost in another world as Eliza gazed at his back. She longed for him to hold her in his arms and tell he everything was at it always had been between them but she felt totally separated from him. She began to appreciate why he had seemed so tired recently. How she wished he could have confided in her.

"Frederic died a terrible death. He had an illness for which there was no cure. He wanted me to end his life for him but I couldn't do that. When I told him I intended to spend the rest of my life with you he gave up his will to live. I suppose you might say that he died from a broken heart."

"When did all this take place?" Eliza asked gently. She felt such compassion for him and wanted to comfort him in his grief although it was something she was finding it very hard to comprehend.

"A few weeks ago. I tried to look after him but the strain became too much for me. I eventually moved him to a nursing home and he died a few days later."

"What of his family? Do they know about all of this?"

"He had a brother whom he never saw and his parents were both dead. He had depended upon me for everything even though he was such a brilliant doctor. He had been like me, poor in pocket but rich in ideas and talent. We had built up a good reputation for ourselves although there were some who disapproved of the type of work we did."

Eliza wanted to ask about the type of work could possibly have caused such consternation but had a feeling she had asked enough for one day. Perhaps one day he would feel able to tell her more.

It was now almost six months since she had left the hospital. She was much stronger and in very little pain. She was getting into the habit of referring to Mac as 'The Doctor' because of the professional ethics surrounding her being one of his patients. Had he not been suffering the trauma of his relationship with Frederic at the same time, he would surely have been able to help Eliza even more.

Since Eliza no longer had need of the care of a nurse, this lady's services were dispensed with. Catriona remained however, to be Eliza's faithful maid.

Eliza continued with her work at her father's studio. Though she no longer felt welcome there since her father disapproved of her continuing relationship with Mac. The visits she made to her mother's house were happy ones although tinged with sadness because her parents could not find it in themselves to share in her happiness. She found it something of a strain spending even a few hours without talking about Mac but that was how it had to be. Her father resented her taking gifts for her parents, saying she was 'salving her conscience'. So she took small gifts for the two girls and her mother, leaving the boys to wonder why they were excluded. She was pleased to see that they were all growing up healthily and enjoyed hearing the news from those who had gone to live overseas. As the years passed, she found herself growing further and further apart from her family although she never forgot them and still visited them whenever possible.

CHAPTER 4

With the passing months, Mac's health deteriorated. He grew weaker and the time he spent either tending his patients or working on research projects became shorter.

Eliza saw all this with an aching heart. She remembered how strong and active he and been until this strange illness afflicted him. No one seemed to understand the nature of his illness and even Mac himself appeared unwilling to discuss it. Eliza desperately wished she could help him. She tried to talk to him about it but he always managed to change the subject. She had a secret suspicion that he was in some way ashamed of the illness. She remembered what he had told her about his colleague. Could this be the same illness? There were times when he seemed to be rallying. For a while he would be his old self again and then Eliza would seize the short periods of happiness. Throughout all of this time, he never forsook his conviction that God was a supernatural creation of superstitious minds. Indeed Eliza herself now felt that were there truly a God, he would not be allowing them to suffer in this way.

Eventually Mac made the decision that it was no longer reasonable for him to try to maintain his practice. Many times he had to send an assistant to tend a sick patient because he himself was too sick to go. Sometimes he did force himself to venture out in the middle of the night to a particularly sick person; but he knew that his own weakness and tiredness could cause him to make wrong decisions which could have tragic consequences.

He made it known at last that he was ceasing to practise medicine in the town and arrangements were made for his competent assistant to take over. His patients were saddened to hear that the doctor's health was forcing him to retire. It gave them no sort of encouragement to realise that the man they had thought was all-powerful had no remedy for his own ills.

It was on a damp misty day that Eliza and Mac, accompanied by their belongings and the ever-faithful Catriona set out to begin a new life together. Eliza was twenty-six and had not lived in her parents' home for some time. She and Mac had discussed the matter of his health and decided that if his life was in danger, which Mac seriously considered to be possible, then they wanted to spend what was left of it together.

Mac had owned property in Southport for many years and now he sold some of this and invested in a large house for them both. When Eliza first saw the house she was transported back to the day when she first visited Mr Larchworth. She had decided there and then that one day she would be mistress of such a grand house and now that dream looked like becoming realised.

It was not merely the house which filled Eliza with delight. It was also the approach and its setting. They travelled down Lord Street, its tree-lined splendour making her gasp. Then they turned into the road where they were to live and soon stopped before the house itself. It stood behind a high wall. They passed through the gate and along the driveway to the front door. Eliza stood for some time gazing up at the façade of the house. There were large square bay windows downstairs, one on either side of the front door. Similar ones graced the upper floor and around the tops of those were decorative battlements, probably giving rise to the house's name 'Castle Bar'. Attic windows filled the top of the house. To one side of the house, a path led down to a coach house behind the property. No longer in use, but a reminder of the grandeur of a previous age.

The years Eliza was to spend there were to be both happy and sad, but that day was to stand out in her memory for the indescribable joy which filled her heart as she arrived to share her life with Mac.

Their lives were now marred only by the increasing severity of Mac's illness. There were days when he could barely rise from his bed and Eliza would spend those days reading to him or writing down the poetry he composed for her.

Their medical friends would visit him often. Eliza was never sure whether they understood exactly what was wrong with him or not. They would talk with him and sometimes one would arrive unexpectedly with some new remedy they hoped might work. Sometimes these would have a slight effect on him and he would be ecstatic in the hope it gave him. However these improvements were usually short lived.

At no times did he falter in his atheism. He was never tempted to turn to a God for help in his troubles. If anything he became even more convinced of the non-existence of a deity, particularly of a loving father deity. His own experience of an earthly father had been a disappointing one and he could not imagine a heavenly one allowing such a one to be his surrogate.

Most of their time was spent indoors as Mac now seemed to lack the enthusiasm to leave the house at all. They sometimes went for short walks along the road to the sea front. There was never much sea to be seen at Southport as it was always very far out in the estuary, but they could smell the sea air and feel the breezes caressing their faces and they always returned home feeling a little more rejuvenated.

Two or three times each year they would take the train to London. They either stayed with friends there or in one of their favourite hotels. They knew many of the eminent surgeons of the day and Eliza knew that if anyone could find a cure for Mac's illness, then one of them surely could.

These visits were becoming less frequent however, since the long train journey proved too tiring for Mac.

It was on one of these visits that they were intrigued to see evidence of the latest London fashion, the bicycle.

This new fashionable mode of transport was rarely seen outside London, but there the parks were filled with both men and women riding their machines.

The invention was instrumental in helping many women to enjoy a freedom they had hitherto been denied. They could travel around town as they wished. They could go unescorted and when in the company of a gentleman they found it unnecessary to be chaperoned. Chaperones were available at a price and some advertised that they could provide their own bicycles.

In London particularly, women were fighting to gain recognition and freedom. Eliza supported the women's movement, knowing only too well how difficult it was for a woman to gain acceptance in a man's world. She herself had defied all the conventions by making her own way in the world. She had lived alone when women were not expected to do so and she had gone against her parents' wishes by setting up home with a man to whom she was not married.

She knew that tongues had wagged and that she was referred to by all kinds of uncomplimentary names, but she was convinced that in time women would gain the right, taken for granted by men, to please themselves.

It delighted Eliza and Mac to stand in the park or along the pavement in town and watch the cyclists go by. They decided that this would be ideal for them. It would enable them to get around the town more easily without Mac becoming too tired.

The Society magazines of the day advertised the latest machines to arrive on the market and so, during a time when Mac's health seemed to be improving, they placed an order for two of the latest models.

When the new machines arrived by carrier, they were to create quite a stir in the conservative town of Southport.

Together they learned to handle the machines and this enabled them to ride out together along the sea front and enjoy the sea air. As he had anticipated, Mac found that he was able to go further on his bicycle than on foot, before tiring.

As the weather grew colder, they enjoyed riding in the crisp air and well wrapped up against the wind, Mac found that the exercise stimulated his body to generate its own warmth. Hardly a day passed when they did not venture out now, whereas before the advent of their bicycles their excursions were few and far between.

Their bicycles were stored in the hallway of the house. Most owners did the same and the bicycles were treated almost as members of the family and were treasured far too highly to be relegated to some outhouse.

And so it was that on Christmas morning of 1898, Eliza and Mac set out on their bicycles on what was to be for them a momentous ride.

Although they had no religious beliefs, Eliza insisted that they celebrate Christmas as far as the giving and receiving of gifts was concerned. She loved to buy presents for her family and for Mac and in return he always bought a small gift for her – a love gift he would call it, rather than a Christmas present.

Mac became quite enraged when he saw people flocking to church on Christmas morning.
'those people never go near a church for the rest of the year' he snarled as he stood looking out of the window watching the people in their dressed in their Sunday best clothes strolling towards the little church at the end of the road.

"What good do they think it is going to do them if they go today?"

Eliza was used to such outbursts and her only concern was that Mac would weaken himself by getting so upset.

"Come along, Eliza" he suddenly said, "we are going for a cycle ride".

Hoping this would take Mac's mind off the matter, Eliza agreed.

They manoeuvred the cycles carefully out of the doorway and down the path. They began to travel slowly down the road. The weather was cold and indeed there had been some snow, which lay frozen in small piles along the sides of the road. The boys of the neighbourhood had been enjoying themselves with snowball fights when the snow was new. Now it had lost its virgin whiteness and had become an ugly unattractive grey.

Eliza had begun to agree with those who had found the long skirts worn by ladies so impractical. Wearing a long heavy black silk dress was no easy matter and she had to be very careful. Some of the fashion magazines had shown pictures of clothes considered to be more appropriate for cycling, but as yet Eliza had not acquired any.

The doctor was riding a little way behind her to ensure her safety, when all at once a small boy of about ten years of age began running along the side of them, laughing and jeering and making uncomplimentary remarks about the couple.

Eliza thought it best to ignore him at first, but suddenly the boy bent down and, picking up a handful of the frozen snow, threw it at Eliza's skirt.

Eliza was stunned that he should treat a lady in that manner. She brought the bicycle to a standstill and stood trying to regain her composure. The doctor meanwhile had seen the incident and given chase. The boy ran for refuge into the arms of an older man, whom Mac assumed was his grandfather. The man stood holding a walking stick in his hand and Mac brought his bicycle to a halt expecting the gentleman to insist that the boy apologizes for his actions. However the man stepped into the road and lifting his stick poked it into Mac's chest. Mac tried to back away but lost his balance. He and his bicycle lay sprawled in the road.

Eliza rode up in great haste and with not a little concern for Mac, who was not strong enough to withstand such treatment.
"What on earth is happening here?" she cried out.
"Oh it is no more than he deserves" shouted the grandfather, still holding tightly to his grandson's arm.
"The likes of you ought to be tarred and feathered and you would be too if I and a lot of people –decent people I mean – around here, had their way".

So saying, he took his grandson by the hand and they turned to walk away. The lad turned and pulled out his tongue at the couple.

"You disgusting child" called out a woman who had been one of a small crowd of onlookers.
The boy's grandfather turned upon hearing this and rounded upon the woman.

"I trust you are not speaking to my grandson" he called.

"I most certainly am" she replied "I have never seen anything so disgraceful in my life. First he calls out rude remarks to the lady who is merely out enjoying the fresh air. Then you knock her husband off his bicycle and then to crown it all, this horrid child is pulling faces as you turn your back."

There were some mutterings in the crowd, some of agreement but a few who obviously thought the pair had been justified in their actions.

As often happened, on such occasions, the local police constable was not long in arriving on the scene.

"Well what have we here?" he asked.

Mac calmly explained to the constable what had taken place and notes were written in the official police notebook. The two perpetrators of the crime stood silently by until they were asked for their names and addresses. Witnesses were also asked to come forward with their details and at this juncture many of them decided that discretion was the better part of valour and drifted away.

Mac, Eliza and the two offenders were asked to accompany the officer to the Police station where they would each be given the opportunity to retail the events as they had happened.

Since Mac's bicycle was now unfit to ride, they asked if they might return their machines to their homes before attending the police station. This request was granted and so by the time they arrived at the station, the two, namely Charles and Thomas Lund had already given their versions of the events and had been charged with assault. All four were informed that they would be required to appear at the Police court on the day following New Year's Day.

Mac and Eliza, still shocked both physically and emotionally by the onset, walked along in silence until they reached the haven of Castle Bar.

The door was opened by Catriona who could only try to imagine what had happened. They could not bring themselves to give her the full details of the incident and once the door was closed they retreated into the drawing room. There at last they held each other close for a long time. Each knew what the other was thinking and feeling and neither knew the right words to say.

It was Mac who finally broke the silence.

"I am so sorry Eliza that I caused this to happen."

"Why have you caused it?" she asked in amazement.

"You heard what the old man said. We are not regarded as decent people because we are not married. You do not deserve that kind of treatment simply because you happen to love a man who has stupid and unacceptable principles."

"Your principles are perfectly acceptable to me my darling and they are far from stupid. Your beliefs are my beliefs and whatever we believe is of no concern to anyone else. You have done more good in your life than most people could even dream of doing and yet you are treated in this despicable manner."

"I love you so much Eliza. I wish I could find a way of showing how much."

"You show me with every breath you take and every word you utter. You have given me more happiness in these past years than most people experience in a lifetime."

They tried to forget the episode but the harsh words of the old man were still ringing in their ears as Catriona came to tell them that their Christmas dinner was ready.

Mac had tried to persuade Eliza and Catriona that Christmas Day was no different from any other day, but he appeared to have failed miserably. Catriona loved to hear tales from Eliza about the latest fashions in London and this year they had decided to decorate a fir tree according to the fashion started by the Queen. Theirs was only a small tree but Catriona made it look quite splendid with its decorations of fruit and sweetmeats.

The two of them walked into the dining room where Catriona had been invited to join them for the meal. She had made a great effort with the table and waited to see their approval. However, such been the effect of the morning's events that neither Eliza nor Mac could he persuaded to join in the Christmas festivities. The meal was conducted in almost total silence. Catriona wished she could be alone with Eliza and possibly find out what had happened. She knew that Eliza had been looking forward eagerly to this day and now something had happened to spoil it for her.

Eliza had loved Christmas as a child. She had loved giving and receiving gifts, singing carols in church and all the other festivities which went along with that time of year. This was the first time she had been apart from her family at Christmas and her emotions were running high as she thought of how she had rejected them and how different her life was likely to be in the future.

The silence was broken by the sound of the bell being rung outside the front door. The maid opened it and they all waited to see whom she would announce.

"There is a police officer at the door, Sir" Catriona said quietly as she entered the dining room. "Shall I ask him to wait until you have finished your meal?"

"No it's all right. I'll come along now. Show him into the drawing room."

Catriona's face was a study as she watched Mac leave the room. Then, alone at last with Eliza, she spied her chance.

"What on earth has happened?" she asked in little more than a whisper.

Eliza was glad to tell someone and she told Catriona as quickly as possible about the boy and his Grandfather. Catriona was shocked but she reassured Eliza quite confidently that no one else shared the old man's views.

The door opened and Mac came into the room looking drawn and tired.

"Eliza, the officer would like to speak to us both. Can you come into the drawing room?"

She wondered what the young officer was thinking as she walked into the room. She was becoming paranoid now, imagining that everyone was considering her to be a wicked woman. She wished the feelings would go away.

"I hope you will not consider it out of place if I advise you that you might consider securing the services of a good Solicitor."

"But why should we need a Solicitor? Surely we have done nothing wrong" Eliza was quite affronted by this suggestion.

"Well you see, the gentleman concerned is quite influential in certain circles and it is likely that he will try to put forward some sort of defence."
Mac almost exploded. "What kind of defence could he possibly put forward? "
"I can't really say, Sir, but I can only advise you both to be prepared for anything".
Mac called for the maid to see the police officer out and then he turned to Eliza.
"There is absolutely no reason why we should need to defend ourselves against this character. He is guilty. There were several witnesses to the attack and we will have no problem in obtaining damages against him."

As far as Mac was concerned, the matter was closed. Until the court case.

It was on the third of January that Mac and Eliza had to appear at the Southport police court to secure convictions against the two. Just as the police officer had suggested he might, the grandfather had obtained a clever defence Lawyer, a Mr F. Jones and Eliza was called into the witness box to testify against the boy.

Confident though Mac was that they would win the day, Eliza felt like a criminal herself as she stepped forward to be questioned. Her lack of composure was not evident. She stood erect and serene as the solicitor faced her.

"Would you mind telling the court exactly what happened on the morning of December 25th as you rode your bicycle along Duke Street?" He appeared quite kind in his manner and Eliza was feeling much calmer as she began to speak.

"The boy had been running alongside me for some distance. I took little notice at first and then he bent down and picked something up which he threw at me."

"And what was that thing that he threw?"

"I think it was some frozen snow. I thought at first it was a stone but it was too soft to have been that."

"I see and where did it hit you?"

"It hit the skirt of my dress and fell to the ground."

"Doing you no harm I trust"

"No physical harm but I was shocked and startled at the act"
"Shocked and startled eh?" She wondered why he had chosen to comment upon her remark. It was one she had made in her statement to the police.

"Why do you think you felt like that?"

"As I said, his action occasioned the shock"

Mr Jones looked around the room, smiled to himself and then turned to Eliza. She was totally unprepared for his next question.

"I believe you are familiarly known as The Woman who Did?

Eliza was stunned. She looked desperately to where Mac was sitting with the Solicitor who was acting on their behalf. This man now stood up.

"Objection!" he called out.
Mr Jones continued with his questioning.

"Are you married to Edward Percy Plantagenet McLoghlin?"

"Objection!"
"I am coming to the question of decency" Mr Jones continued.

Objection was made yet again but Mr Jones was not going to be deterred by these objections.
"Are you the wife of Edward Percy Plantagenet McLoghlin?"

Eliza waited for the objection to be made, but none came. She realised that the question could not be avoided any longer.

"In the best and truest sense I am" She said proudly.

There was a gasp among the observers assembled in the courtroom.

"But you have not been married to him?"

"I am not legally married to him – no"

"And are you not shocked and startled by that?"

Eliza had had quite enough of this line of questioning and replied
"Not at all, but Dr McLoghlin is present in court and I think he is the best person to answer that question."

"But I would just as soon have you answer it"

Mr Hodge, Mac's solicitor who had raised several objections throughout this line of questioning, now stood up.

"No doubt you would, but I suggest that Miss Millard has stood quite enough of your insulting questions and as she says 'why not ask the doctor to answer?'"

The Magistrates agreed to this request and Mac entered the witness box.

Mr Jones stepped forward.

"I do not consider that this man is a fit person to answer questions in this court. He is living with Miss Millard without being married to her and I refuse to ask him any questions at all"

Mac wanted the chance to speak up for Eliza and himself but realised he was being denied his chance.

The Magistrates conferred and then spoke:
"We find the defendants guilty as follows:
Charles Lund - you are guilty of assaulting Miss Eliza Millard and are therefore fined the sum of two shillings and sixpence including costs; William Lund – you are found guilty of assaulting Edward Percy Plantagenet McLoghlin and are fined the sum of two shillings and

sixpence, plus the cost of repairs to the bicycle, which shall not exceed five pounds."

Mac and Eliza had won the case but felt as though they had lost. They had had no opportunity to dispute the aspersions cast upon their characters.

On his return home, still deeply distressed, Mac sat down to write a letter to the local paper.

"I desire to make a statement in your columns with reference to the proceedings at the police court this morning in the case of the successful prosecution of William and Charles Lund by Miss Eliza Millard and myself.
The utter failure of the attempt on the part of Mr Jones, the Solicitor for the defence, to impeach our veracity because we do not hold the vulgar or usually accepted views upon the question of marriage is the first point to which I wish to draw attention. I know nothing of Mr Jones' previous professional conduct but feel sure that the majority both of his own profession and the educated public will sufficiently stigmatize his behaviour this morning in deliberately insulting a lady by asking her questions on matters purely private and personal and which had not the remotest connection with the defence in which he was professionally engaged. That he failed in his purpose is sufficiently indicated by the decision of the Magistrates"

He went on in his letter to explain his views on marriage and to explain that neither he nor Eliza wished to force their views on to the world where, he maintained:
'that men and women are far too uncivilised as yet to be ready for sexual freedom'.

"We have always considered our relationship as only concerning ourselves and always treated it as such. Nevertheless, both of us have the greatest detestation of falsehood in any form and we have always

97

openly repudiated any inference that our relationship was other than it is one of absolute mutual freedom.

"as we are both entirely independent of the world and, as a matter of fact, care nothing whatever for the opinion of the world on any point so far as it concerns only ourselves, we should not have troubled you with what we still maintain is only private and personal. However we do not wish the principle involved in sexual freedom, which certainly does concern the world to be misjudged and misinterpreted should the cowardly cross-examination of Mr Jones be held to denote it. To prevent this, I will write down clearly and briefly what principles are really concerned.

the only possible basis for a just and righteous sex-relationship is the presence of the greatest amount of sexual attraction of which the two persons involved are capable and, on the other hand, the absence of any mercenary motive whatever.

It is impossible for any ceremony, religious, civil or legal to create or call into being these desirable elements or maintain them in being where they already exist.

That the resources of those persons who enter into such a sex-relationship as that defined above shall be sufficient and so disposed as to render each of the persons concerned absolutely free from dependence upon the other in any sense of the term. That this arrangement is primary, unconditional and absolute.

In conclusion I will point out that we believe in marriage just in the same sense as we believe in workhouses for paupers, gaols for criminals and crutches for cripples. When there are neither criminals, cripples nor paupers, such arrangements will not be necessary."

The Southport Visiter of January 4th published Mac's statement and he was pleased that he had at least had the opportunity of explaining his views. He had not realised however that the reporting of the case was not confined to the local press. A report appeared in other papers, some quite far afield. There was obviously a shortage of news around the Christmas holiday period and other newspapers had seized upon the story as being one which might sell a few copies.

On January 11th a reply was published, received from a man who had read the report in a Yorkshire weekly paper.

"It would appear as though a youth had assaulted a doctor and a lady because the latter had the presumption to cohabit without prior ceremonial. It is gratifying to observe that the Magistrates of sunny Southport were not so dazzled by the logic of the young gentleman of ten and his grandfather as to dismiss the case. This gentleman of ten may not have known that unmarried wives had a right to cycle but the elder gentleman ought not only to have known this but might have been expected to have anticipated he would have had to learn a little more if he tried the experiment of converting them to a belief in matrimony by the expedient of bicycle breaking"

When Mac and Eliza read this they laughed together. It took away all the grief of the past weeks, because they knew that there were other people in the world who agreed with them and who would see the actions of that solicitor as an intrusion in their private beliefs and values.

Several replies appeared in the paper in the next weeks, all condemning the actions of the Solicitor and offering support and sympathy.

They were congratulated on their 'Bravery'

One correspondent wrote that
"Savagely ignorant and acrimonious attack of the Solicitor Jones upon your private union"
was
"the most insolently audacious violation of personal right I have ever read or heard of"

Another writer wrote:

"I am glad to see you have successfully asserted your just claims and that magistrates have upheld you to a certain extent in your endeavour to resist the introduction of irrelevant matter, intended merely to prejudice your case and to deny the common rights of citizenship to heterodox thinkers. I wish I could do something to ventilate the matter in the London papers…. In the South at least we are now in a backwater and must wait till the current changes before we can do anything in this movement for freedom."

Eliza and Mac regarded these letters as sufficient proof that they did not stand alone and hoped that it was a page of history that was now closed.

Throughout recent months they had wondered why Eliza was being referred to as The Woman Who Did. Did what? She would ask Mac.

Eventually they discovered the reason. A young unmarried English couple had emigrated to Canada to set up life together. They soon had two children and their lives were complete. However, the man was taken ill and died. The woman, not wishing to remain in Canada without him, decided to return to England with her children. The Authorities deemed this to be illegal. She could return but could not bring the children who were Canadian citizens and had no father to accompany them. The case received much coverage and she became known as The Woman Who Did. This was now the reason that people were putting that title upon Eliza.

CHAPTER 5

Eliza loved to visit her parents whenever the opportunity arose. However, Mac was not welcome there and she never liked to leave him alone for long. When she did go home she tried to ensure that her father was not there so that she and her mother could talk together as they had done many years earlier. Susannah was torn between her loyalty to her husband and her love for her daughter. James told her how she should think and what she should believe. She loved all her children but her husband was the person to whom she must look for material support. Eliza wanted her mother to understand that Mac was a wealthy man who would always be happy to help her mother and father if they needed financial support. But she was sure that her parents would be too proud to accept money from the man of whom they disapproved so strongly.

Once the excitement had died down over the assault episode, it began to torment Mac that he really was creating an intolerable burden for Eliza to bear by refusing to allow them to be married.

His principles were strong and he would not suggest marriage to Eliza and yet he hated to think of her running the gauntlet of abuse once he was no longer there to protect her. A year had passed and yet he still remembered vividly the pain that had been caused and he wanted desperately to safeguard her from a repetition of that. The difficulties encountered by the couple who had emigrated to Canada seemed to be a warning to them.

Mac's illness had always been one which seemed to disappear for long periods of time and then return with an increased severity. Now it returned with different and more distressing symptoms. He was stricken with paralysis. Although he felt little pain, he sometimes found it almost impossible to lift his arms in the morning and he needed help with washing and dressing. The indignity of this caused him more distress than any of the other results of the illness. It had been a long time now since he had been able to use his bicycle and the two machines were relegated to an outbuilding. At times he appeared to be near to death, unable to speak or hear for a while. Then just as suddenly he would recover and for some time he would have no symptoms whatsoever.

He was anxious that should one of his relapses prove fatal, his affairs should be quite in order so that Eliza should experience no financial problems. He knew that should the paralysis become permanent, he would be unable to sign documents and so he decided that as a matter of urgency he needed to consult a solicitor and have his Will reviewed so as to ensure that everything he possessed was left to Eliza and that she should have no problems regarding the administration of his estate.

However, he had another request which he needed to discuss with her. He had secretly cherished a wish that some of his money be bequeathed to the Royal College of Surgeons of England, for the financing of a scholarship. He knew how much easier his own life would have been if he could have had the benefit of financial assistance. His idea was that a scholarship be awarded to a boy from his home town of Wigan, who although well gifted intellectually so that the academic demands made on him would not be beyond him, he should be of such a lowly background that his family could not afford to finance him. He did not know how to provide such a scholarship and did not want to do so at the expense of Eliza's well-being. He was well aware that he might predecease her by many years and might need the money for herself. He preferred that she should benefit primarily from his fortune but decided to discuss his private dream with her.

Eliza thought this a splendid idea. She was more than happy for Mac to include this bequest in his Will but he would not hear of it.

"No," he insisted, "this is a dream of mine but one which might cause you financial hardship. It must remain a dream, unless of course you wish to include it in your own Will."

Eliza had no money of her own and few personal possessions other than her clothes and jewellery. She saw no need to write a will yet but made a conscious decision that if Mac were to die and she were to inherit his fortune, then she would need to make a will and this would include the bequest he so desired.

Mac's brother was now married and his wife was expecting their first child. Very occasionally they would visit Mac and Eliza but made it obvious that they were both embarrassed by and disapproving of their circumstances.

As a consequence, it was a very solitary life they led in Southport. Their real friends, the ones whom they trusted, were in London. Mac called upon his Solicitor friend to draw up his will and his doctor friends for advice with regard to his increasingly severe illness.

Nursing Mac as she had done for so many years had taken its toll of Eliza's physical and emotional strength. She began to write her own poetry as an outlet for her pent-up feelings, but she was almost ashamed to let Mac read her attempts, because they compared so unfavourably with his own for fluency and expression. Nevertheless she found it immensely satisfying to write for her own pleasure and the doctor loved whatever she wrote because it came from her heart.

They loved their now less frequent visits to London and it was early in the New Year that they decided to take the train there and visit those professional friends whom they might soon find it impossible to visit, once his condition worsened.

When they arrived at the Thackeray Hotel in Great Russell Street the proprietor greeted them like old friends and showed them to their room in the newly installed lift.

They spent the first few days relaxing and renewing old acquaintances. They contacted their friends, many of whom were in the legal and medical professions.

Mac had made an appointment to see Henry Morris, a consultant surgeon whose rooms were in Cavendish Square. At the appointed time, Eliza and Mac arrived and were shown into the lavish waiting room. Eliza tried to conceal the nervousness she felt about the possible outcome of the visit.

Henry Morris had been a friend of the couple for many years. They both trusted his judgement and professionalism and had already agreed that whatever his prognosis, they would use it as a basis upon which to plan their future lives.

After a very thorough examination, the surgeon sat at his desk and although he held his pen in a writing position, he did not put pen to paper. Eliza suspected that this was the procrastination process. It was obvious that he was unhappy about voicing his opinions and this could only mean that they would be unpleasant and distressing to hear. She decided that she would have to step in and resolve the situation for everyone concerned.

"If you do not think that Mac will ever regain full health again, please say so. We need to make plans and until we know what the future might hold we cannot plan anything at all."

Mac felt so weak that he just sat motionless in his chair and marvelled at the strength this woman was showing at a time when her heart must be breaking.

"Oh dear, there really is no way of making this easy for either of us" Henry Morris got up from his chair and walked around the desk.

"We both know the history of your illness. We both know how you contracted it"   .
Eliza was stunned. Who were the 'both' to whom he referred?

"All I can say to you is that you should take each day as it comes. You could find the attacks becoming less frequent. On the other hand you must be prepared for the worst."

He saw them to the door. It was difficult for a doctor to deliver such news as this at any time, but to a friend it was heartbreaking.

Eliza and Mac returned to the hotel and determined that come what may, they would not let the doctor's words spoil what might be their last visit to London.

Two of Mac's medical friends joined them for dinner and the evening began pleasantly enough. The conversation was stimulating and although on such occasions Eliza felt quite inadequate, she loved to hear the learned men discussing matters of such great importance to them.

She could not rid her mind, though, of the fact that Dr Morris had said they both knew how the illness had started. She knew she had to discuss this once she and Mac were alone, but they never seemed to be alone these days.
Suddenly, one of the men looked towards Eliza and said quite unexpectedly, "Why don't the two of you get married?"

Mac was astonished. Surely his friends were familiar enough with his views to realise that such a suggestion would be unthinkable. However since he had been tormented by the very possibility himself he was rather sharper in his reaction than he might otherwise have been.

"Lionel, I hope that was some kind of tasteless joke."

"No Mac, I must apologise, it has been in my head for so long that I must have assumed that you knew what I was thinking. What concerns me is what might happen to Eliza if you should die. We have to be truthful, there is every possibility that you might go quite suddenly and how would she fare?"

"No problem there, Lionel" Mac smiled smugly. "I have taken great care to word my will in such a way that she would receive everything I have".

"That is all very well, but if your brother should dispute the will, she might very probably end up with nothing at all."

It was something Mac had never even considered. He had left a small sum to his brother and he was sure his brother would understand but he knew what Lionel meant. People did strange things over wills. Why anyone should believe themselves to have a right to anyone else's money or possessions was beyond his comprehension. His brother had his own inheritance from their father and he was sure he would be happy for Eliza to inherit the money.

Nevertheless the idea cast a cloud over the rest of the evening and when Mac and Eliza retired to bed it was inevitable that the subject should be discussed further. Indeed over the next few days they hardly talked of anything else. It was perfectly true that Eliza would not win a contest over Mac's will. Even wives often had to justify their right to a husband's money; she would just not stand a chance.

The anxiety which this question caused resulted in Mac being stricken with one of the severest attacks he had hitherto experienced. He could hardly move a muscle and lay, barely conscious in the hotel room where he was visited by the doctor called by Eliza. He was too ill to return home and always the question of Eliza's inheritance was on his lips. He called her to him.

"I am sure I am about to die, my dearest love. I know that to be true and I cannot bear to lose you but this time I feel there is little hope. I would like you to call the registrar and have him perform a marriage ceremony. This is the last and most honourable thing I can do" his words were but a whisper.

Eliza was in torment. Things always appear worse during the night and that night seemed endless. Sitting there in that familiar hotel room she felt like a stranger. The doctors remained by his side, feeling as helpless as she did. Occasionally his hand would stir in hers and she would bend to put her ear to his lips to catch what it was that he was trying to say. It was always the same. "Marriage" – the very sacrament against which he had preached for so long. As dawn broke and the noises of the London streets reached their ears, he seemed slightly improved. His words were still inaudible but his fever had subsided and he was more conscious of people around him. Once again he whispered the word 'Registrar'.

The doctor with whom they had dined the night they arrived in London was visiting at the time. He turned to Eliza and said "I am sure that if you contact the Registrar now, he will make the necessary arrangements for your marriage, if of course that is what you have decided to do"

Eliza was distraught. She had secretly longed for this moment for so long. Now that it was a real possibility, she did not know how she should react. If she agreed too readily, Mac might think that she had never really agreed with his views. If she did not concur with his wishes then he might die and it would be too late.

She sat by his bedside and took hold of both his hands.

"Please give me some sign that you are absolutely certain that you want to go through with this"

Mac was more certain of this than he had ever been of anything. What use were principles when the person you loved was likely to suffer because of them. He struggled desperately to say what he felt. All he could do was nod and squeeze Eliza's hand.

The doctor suggested that he should be the one to seek out a Registrar and request that he perform the ceremony as soon as possible. Eliza thanked him profusely and she could tell that Mac would want to do the same. He promised to see to the matter as soon as he could that very day. Eliza escorted him out of their hotel room and watched from the window as he disappeared across the square. The rest of that morning passed in silence. Both Mac and Eliza were contemplating what was to change both in their circumstances and in their status in society. They were going to become respectable. Eliza wondered what difference this would make to her relationship with her father. She wondered whether she should even tell them. If they could not accept her decisions and principles before, then she did not want them to bother doing so now.

The following day the Doctor came to see them with the news that they would need to obtain a Registrar General's licence in order to marry. They had already been in London for some days and the wedding could take place as soon as they liked. However, Eliza would have to present herself at the Register Office to lodge the request for the marriage. Because of the state of Mac's health it was not feasible for him to do it himself. The doctor said he would escort Eliza to see the Registrar that very afternoon. He was as good as his word. Soon after luncheon was over, he arrived in his carriage and Eliza embarked on the journey which was to change her life.

Emanuel Newbery, the Registrar, was kindness itself. He had obviously been briefed as to the delicacy of the situation and he took Eliza through all the necessary documentation which went along with obtaining the licence.

They needed to have two witnesses to the marriage, and this she would discuss with Mac.

When she returned to the hotel, Mac was awake and ready to hear all that had happened. It was amazing how his condition could improve in such a short period of time. She explained what had transpired and that they would need two witnesses. Mac was more concerned at this time however in persuading Eliza to go out and buy a new dress. Eliza did not relish the idea of doing this alone. If only her sister or her mother could go with her. If only Catriona was there. Sometimes she did accompany them on their visits to London and she always felt very excited at being invited. This time however she had asked if she might spend the time with her own family. They had not seen much of her recently and both Eliza and Mac felt this would be an ideal opportunity for her to visit them. The hotel proprietor had recommended to them a woman who lived nearby, who might be a suitable companion for Eliza. She proved to be a pleasant enough person and trustworthy in the extreme but she was a stranger to Eliza and this was the kind of occasion which you did not wish to share with strangers. She decided to go alone.

Putting on her hat and coat she kissed Mac tenderly. He took her hand in his and with a tremor in his voice he said "Pink Roses". Eliza's heart sang and she smiled at his thoughtfulness.
She had no heart for this shopping trip. Walking along the High Street she stopped at the first window which caught her eye. In the centre of the window was a mannequin dressed in a heavy pink silk dress. It had a high frilled neckline, a tight waist and a bustle at the back. It was ideal. Eliza entered the shop and asked to be shown the dress. It was expensive but that was of little consequence. The shop assistant thought Eliza looked magnificent in the dress and in the hat which was produced to accompany it. However, Eliza had little interest in the outfit except that Mac had wanted her to buy it and he would want her to look her best. How often she had dreamed of her wedding day and now it had arrived it counted among the saddest of her life.

She arranged for the package to be delivered to the Hotel and proceeded to find a florist's shop.

She asked for a bouquet of pink roses to be delivered to the hotel the following morning. Her next mission was to find a jeweller's shop. Now she had much more interest in her purchase. She selected a beautiful gold watch chain as her wedding gift to Mac. She asked that it be engraved with the words 'For all Eternity' and for that also to be delivered to the hotel.

Her shopping completed, Eliza hurried back along the street and up the steps of the hotel. She almost leaped up the stairs and did not stop until she reached their room.

Mac's face lit up with pleasure as she entered the room. He was sitting up in bed and had eaten a light meal. His voice however, was barely audible and his words were rather confused. Frustration caused him to sigh and lie back on his pillows with closed eyes. Then he reached on to the bedside table and took up a small package. He handed it silently to Eliza. She opened it and gasped to see that it contained a wedding ring. How had he acquired that? She wondered.

He smiled as he saw the curiosity on her face and then he closed his eyes and slept.

The following morning, the sixteenth of March, eighteen hundred and ninety nine dawned crisp, cold and bright. Spring was on its way. Crocuses pushed their way through the damp soil around the London squares. This was a time for new life, not a time for death. Eliza stared out of the window on to the scene outside. People were going about their daily business as though this was just another ordinary day. As though it were not the end of an era and the beginning of she knew not what.

How would Mac come to terms with having betrayed his long held principles about the futility, nay the immorality even, of marriage? She had helped in this betrayal and she wondered if she would ever be able to forgive herself. He had done it for her, she knew that, and she had allowed him to do it.

The maid had brought her breakfast to her room that morning. She had not slept in Mac's room since he had become so ill. She knew he needed to be alone.

"Do you know what day it is today, Francis?" she asked of the maid.

"Wednesday, I think Ma'am" she replied as she went about her tasks of tidying the room.

"Yes but do you know what is special about today?"

"No, Ma'am"

"It is my wedding day. The happiest day in a woman's life. Not mine however, because my husband-to-be is dying. He is marrying me because he is dying. Can you imagine how sad that makes me?"

Francis stopped in her tracks and turned to Eliza.

"Oh Ma'am, I am so sorry. I always imagined that you and the doctor were already married. I never realised. I am so sorry."

"Please don't be sorry. This is how he wants it to be. I must try to be happy for his sake. Could you please do something very important for me?"

"If I can, what would you like me to do?"

"Would you come with me and be my witness? We have a doctor to be one of the witnesses but I would like you to be the other one. I have no other woman I can ask"

Francis looked down at the ground. Then she looked up and said shyly, "I have no proper wedding clothes to wear. I would be a disgrace to you dressed like this." She held out the poor thin dress she was wearing under her apron.

"That is no problem, Francis, You are about the same size as me and I have more dresses than I could possibly ever wear. Choose one from my wardrobe now"

Together the two women looked through Eliza's wardrobe until they selected a pale blue one which Francis particularly admired. Eliza had worn it one day when Francis had first met her and she had thought it the most beautiful dress in the world.

"You must wear it and then you must keep it as my gift to you" Eliza loved giving presents to people and she particularly loved seeing other women share in the happiness she felt herself. She never thought that men appreciated gifts the way women did. How she wished she could have had a daughter to lavish gifts upon.

Francis could barely contain her happiness. Then she realised with shame that this was a sad occasion and perhaps she should not allow herself such elation.

Francis had helped Eliza put on the new dress she had bought the previous day. They arranged the hat and its delicate veil and Eliza chose her favourite jewellery. Then she helped Francis to dress. She was a pretty young lady and the dress suited her well.

Now Eliza stood gazing out of the window, imagining the beginning of her new life. She saw the florist's delivery girl step up to the door of the hotel and waited for her to climb the stairs and knock on their door.

Francis went to open it and took from her the beautiful bouquet of pink roses. Eliza took some coins from her purse and gave them to the girl for delivering them so carefully. The girl looked up into Eliza's face and saw the sadness there. She took the coins graciously but wondered why someone so rich and beautiful could be so sad on her wedding day.

Still Mac had not seen Eliza that morning. Since they were to travel together in the Hansom cab, it was impossible for him not to see her before the wedding, but she would try to keep her appearance a mystery for as long as she could.

Lionel arrived to help Mac to dress for the ceremony. Eliza had laid out his clothes the night before and hoped she had forgotten nothing.

Lionel kissed Eliza lightly on the cheek and then went to assist Mac to sit on the edge of the bed while he was helped on with his clothes.

When he was quite ready, Lionel went to the door to inform Eliza that they were ready. She decided it was time now to reveal herself to Mac. She knocked on his door and went in. His eyes filled with tears when he saw how beautiful she looked. He stretched his arms weakly towards her and tried to speak. It was an effort and the words, when they came, made little sense. However, Eliza and Mac did not need words to express their love for each other. They held each other closely. Then Eliza opened her purse and took out the little package she had been waiting to give him. He did not have the strength even to unwrap it and so she did this for him. When he saw the watch chain and read its inscription, his eyes filled with tears once again. She gently wiped them away with her dainty handkerchief and then arranged the watch chain along the front of his coat. Lionel had told them that the cab would he here at 9:45. The porter would come up to tell them of its arrival and would help to get Mac into the chair and down to the lift. There was time for Lionel to congratulate Eliza on her wonderful appearance and to wish the couple as much happiness as possible in the circumstances. There there was a knock on the door, the porter announced the arrival of the cab and he and Lionel prepared Mac. They were grateful for the lift as they manoeuvred the chair into it and closed the heavy iron gates. Eliza and Frances did not accompany them for fear of overloading the lift. They went down the two flights of stairs and waited for them at the bottom. Frances was feeling more than a little self-conscious as the other chamber-maids saw her in her finery.

It was a short journey to the Register Office, no more than walking distance but the cab took the journey at a slow pace to avoid giving Mac any more discomfort than was necessary. Once there, a wheelchair was provided to take Mac inside and the cab driver was asked to return in half an hour.

It was a civil ceremony with no religious rites. They made their vows to each other and the register was signed. Edward Percy Plantaganet Macloghlin, aged 43 years, Bachelor. Profession – Retired Physician. Retired maybe but as long as he had breath in his body he would never retire from helping the sick. Their residence was recorded as the Thackeray Hotel.

Eliza signed her name, Eliza Millard, for the last time. A spinster, aged 35 years. She had no profession to record but saw her father's name and his profession – Photographic Artist. A pang of sorrow gripped her as she wished that her parents could have been here on her wedding day.

Mac took the ring from its case and slipped it on to Eliza's finger. They both knew that this was not a symbol of her belonging to him but of a shared understanding of the reasons they had embarked on this act.

After the ceremony they left as they had arrived. Mac was carried and Eliza walked behind to the cab. She knew that the rest of her life would now be devoted to carrying out his wishes. She wondered what lay in store for them. How long would they enjoy wedded bliss and what would her life be like after he had gone?

After the wedding, Mac remained desperately ill for many weeks. They stayed in the hotel because there seemed no point in moving out. He was obviously too ill to undertake the long journey back to Southport and since he was beyond medical help there was no need for him to go into hospital. To Eliza it seemed to be merely a matter of time.

However he did not die. He totally lost his power of speech and could barely walk for much of the time, but he did not die. Eliza knew that as long as he was alive there was hope that he might make a full recovery and her medical friends confirmed this. She still kept in her heart the mystery of what the doctor had said – that they 'both' knew how this had happened. She never mentioned it to Mac or to anyone else.

At the beginning of June it was decided that they could now return to Southport. He was fully conscious and apart from his lack of speech, had no outward signs of his illness.

On the night before they left, Lionel Shepherd came round to the hotel and they had dinner together. Mac was able to write messages on a pad and in this way they were able to enjoy a lively if somewhat strange conversation. Before he left, Lionel mentioned the fact that he was delighted that they had decided to get married after all.

"I am sure that in time you will see that you have taken the right course of action. It may not seem so now but I can assure you that Eliza's life will be simplified a hundredfold in the event of your passing. It is strange but true that the possession of a piece of paper can alter your entire life."

He turned to leave but Eliza's thoughts were racing.

"Piece of paper?" she asked "what piece of paper?"

"Why, the marriage certificate of course, surely you haven't lost it so soon?"

"Lost it, no, how could I? I never had it to lose"

They realised that in the circumstances surrounding the ceremony, with Mac needing to be carried to the waiting taxi cab, they had completely forgotten to collect the certificate.

"Never fear, I will collect a copy for you tomorrow. I suggest, Mac that you get two copies, and lodge one with your Will."

So saying, Lionel left. He promised to return before they left the following day with the Marriage Certificates. Eliza wondered how she would have managed without Lionel. She wondered how she would manage once Mac finally did leave her. Would there always be a Lionel for her to rely on or would she have to learn to make her own decisions and organise her own life.

CHAPTER 6

Once they had returned to Southport life seemed much easier for them. They had their own possessions around them and Mac was able to walk out into his garden without having to go down several flights of stairs. One of the ground floors was converted into a bedroom for them so that there was no need for him to negotiate stairs at all.

Mac never regained his speech but in every other respect he appeared to the outsider to be quite well. Eliza however knew this not to be the case. He was often in pain, although the source of his pain could not always be traced. He suffered bouts of paralysis which became increasingly more prolonged as his illness progressed.

As Eliza had predicted, he never forgot those whom he considered to be even less fortunate than himself and when other doctors called to ask his opinions about cases that were worrying them, he would listen intently to the description of the symptoms and would think what might be done. Then taking the pen and paper which were always close to his hand he would proceed to suggest remedies. In this way he continued to help the needy long after no help was forthcoming for his own illness. Eliza had never known anyone so brave or so thoughtful for others, even in his own dire circumstances. He seemed to be waiting for death to come and rescue him from this life which had become so intolerable.

During this time, Eliza kept in touch with her parents as well as she could. She rarely left Mac's side and only when his own brother came to visit would she leave him in order to travel to Wigan to visit her family.

On one of her visits she learned that her brother Charles was planning to be married in the Parish Church. The wedding was to be a lavish affair since the bride belonged to a wealthy family. Eliza declined the invitation to attend since she knew Mac would not be well enough to accompany her and she had no intention of giving her family the satisfaction of seeing her attend alone. She decided to send a gift and chose a small silver dish which she thought would not be considered too ostentatious. The wedding was reported in great detail in the local newspaper. Susannah proudly sent a copy for Eliza to read. It described the bride's 'tasteful' white muslin dress with lace flounces, the black dresses worn by the two mothers, Mrs Millard and Mrs Riding, the sumptuous repast held in a local hostelry and a list of wedding gifts. Eliza scanned these with interest, there were oil paintings, engravings, hand-painted fire screens and money from parents and brothers, a book rack containing Byron's works and a satin glove case from her sisters. No mention was made of Eliza's silver dish. She realised that marrying Mac had made no difference to their attitude towards her. She was going to be regarded as an evil woman to her dying day. Only her mother and her sisters seemed to accept her. The men of the family shunned her whenever possible. Eliza tore up the newspaper and threw it into the fire in a rage.

After that she made little attempt to communicate with her family. Occasionally her sisters Margaret and Beatrice would visit her but they felt uncomfortable when they realised that Mac was unable to communicate and they rarely stayed long. Only her brother Edward remained truly loyal to her. He would call whenever he had the opportunity and tell her all that was happening in the studio. He was working there now with his father and was quite excited to report that his father had applied for a patent for some of the improvements he had made in photographic cameras. His most recent invention was the instantaneous shutter and advertisements for the product appeared in local magazines.
Eliza enjoyed Edward's visits and wished that all her brothers could be as understanding as he was.

Mac's condition was worsening rapidly now and Eliza had to prepare herself for the end. She really believed that she was as ready to accept death as he was. She knew it would mean the end of his suffering but she hated the finality which his beliefs placed on his death. If he believed in Eternal Life then she could hold on to the hope of their meeting again one day but his belief was in Eternal Death.

When paralysis finally overcame Mac completely, Eliza was distraught. Holding him close, she kissed him endlessly, refusing to let him go in case death crept in and took him from her.

"Stay with me even so. I want your eyes and mouth if I must lose everything else."

The poetry she wrote to help her through those last dark days were filled with pleading that he should not go, or that she should die in his place. "What if you cannot speak, I shall see all you say"

It was in April 1904 that Death finally won.

Mac had indicated precisely the kind of funeral he wanted. There was to be no form of religious ceremony and her requested that his body be cremated. This in itself was quite unorthodox and had only become legal two years earlier. There were only two crematoria in the country, one in Golders Green in London and the other, a privately owned on in Didsbury, Manchester. Southport was some fifty miles drive from Didsbury but Eliza decided that the journey must be made.

She invited Catriona and two other close friends to accompany her and the coffin on the long journey by horse-drawn hearse. As the hearse drew up outside the house in Leyland Road in Southport, neighbours peered from behind their curtains to see the departure of this strange unorthodox man. The coffin was carried from the house covered in pink roses and leaves and was followed by Eliza, looking beautiful in mourning black. The three other members of the funeral party followed at a short distance, not wishing to intrude upon this private moment.

Hardly a word was spoken as the carriages trundled slowly down the road along tree-lined Lord Street. The spring buds were on the trees and there was a hint of rain in the air. The party travelled for some

118

thirty miles before resting for the night at an inn. The following day the journey was resumed and they reached Didsbury Crematorium in early afternoon. None of the party had ever been to a Cremation before and none knew quite what to expect. Catriona had expected to see the coffin consumed by flames but there was none of this. In accordance with Mac's express wishes, the proceedings were conducted in total silence. What more was there to be said? He had insisted. The coffin stood on a raised altar-like structure, the pink roses still covering it reminding Eliza of the pink roses that had attended the most important moments of their love-marriage. These would be the ones to go with him into the furnace and be the first ones to feel the heat.

Once they were all assembled, a curtain was drawn across in front of the coffin, and Mac was gone. Eliza stared in disbelief at the closed curtain. She wanted to tear them apart and hold Mac in her arms for ever but she knew he had gone and now there were other things she had to do for him.

The party did not return to Southport by road. It had been a long journey and one they had only undertaken out of deference to Mac's wishes. They returned to Southport by train. Eliza was much more composed in the way back. She was able to talk about her plans for her future and the others sensed a kind of relief that it was over.

The words which kept echoing over and over in her head however were the ones she wrote in a poem:

'Dead for Eternity'
'Dead on a silver cloud, floating to far away
Love in a silver shroud, dead and at peace for aye
Life with her sweet head bowed
Grief come to stay – to stay'

Throughout the many years of her relationship with Mac, Eliza had had cause to be grateful to him for helping her to curb a violent temper. After her hysterectomy the tempers had become more violent and Mac had explained to her that it was an unfortunate result of the hormonal

119

imbalance which had resulted from her loss of ovarian function. He had learned to expect the regular outbursts but was often frustrated in his attempts to deal with them. Love and understanding were the only remedies he could prescribe and they seemed to work. The problem was that should any kind of challenge present itself to Eliza at such times, she was totally incapable of dealing with it rationally. The result was often disastrous as far as friendships were concerned. Events which might have given Eliza minor irritation at any other time would become major incidents at these times.

Now these violent outbursts seemed to her friends to be worse than ever. She appeared to be angry that Mac had been taken from her and without him she could not deal with her own anger.   Almost immediately after the funeral Eliza plunged herself into a frenzy of activity.   She cleaned the house from top to bottom and collected together every word that Mac had ever written. He had been writing poetry since he was about eleven years of age, when this had been the only outlet for his emotions. She decided that all his poetry should be kept together and she arranged for them to be printed privately. The completed book was to be entitled Poetry. Her own contribution to the book was a series of poems dealing with her feelings surrounding his paralysis and her own widowhood.

In the introduction she wrote

"Memorial to a child"
...one feels the little hand, the dear little hand
Confiding and craving a responsive clasp.
The little life with mind so big already
Appealing in vain for help and comfort from a mother
who, had she been fond and good and wise
would have cherished her wonderful baby
but they laughed at his wanting to be loved...

The casket containing Mac's ashes had been delivered to her soon after the funeral. Engraved upon the front were the words 'For all Eternity' just as they had been on his watch chain, her wedding gift to him. The casket stood now on the table in her drawing room, always covered in pink roses and waiting for the day when she would give it its final resting place. Before that, however, she had other things to do.

Mac's will had been read in which everything was left to her. She knew that she was now an extremely wealthy woman. In fact she had never realised during Mac's lifetime just how wealthy he was. He had stocks and shares as well as a great deal of property.

She wondered how she could put this new found wealth to the greatest use so that it would serve as a memorial to Mac. She remembered the suggestion he had made for the creation of a scholarship to the Royal College of Surgeons. This was something she could now initiate.

Only two months after Mac's death, Eliza wrote a letter to the Royal College of Surgeons giving them notice that upon her own death she would like a scholarship to be awarded in his memory.

She stipulated that it should be awarded only to young men from Wigan, between the ages of seventeen and a half and twenty-three years who might otherwise suffer the financial hardship which Mac had suffered in his youth. She also stipulated that the young men concerned must be hardworking, of satisfactory conduct and willing to study hard to take advantage of this financial assistance. It was, in short to be awarded to a boy from Wigan who was poor in pocket, but rich in intellect. Her offer was received with much gratitude and the legal advisers of the College were only too pleased to be able to assist in drawing up the details.

However, Eliza's thoughts raced on. Whenever they had been to London, Mac had taken her to the Royal College of Surgeons which he regarded as something of a shrine to the great medical brains which had gone before. There were busts of many of them around the entrance hall and he would take her round and tell her in something resembling awe, of what these great men had achieved. If Mac had not believed in a Spiritual God, he certainly had seen in these men the inspiration he needed to spur him on to greater works for the good of humanity.

Eliza now knew what she must do with at least some of Mac's legacy. She would commission a memorial to him. It would stand in that Hall at the Royal College of Surgeons of England along with the men he so greatly admired. Not only that, but Mac's ashes would be placed in the memorial so that he could spend the Eternity of which he was now part, in the place he loved.

Hardly had the Trustees had time to digest the generosity of this unknown lady from Wigan, than another letter arrived from her. This time she was also offering them the memorial to Mac. This posed something of a problem to the Trustees because such honours were usually reserved for the great and the good of the land and not for some unknown doctor from Wigan. As if anticipating their hesitation, Eliza outlined her doctor's achievements. He had received his medical education at Liverpool University where he had gained several distinctions. In 1882 he had been awarded the Bligh Gold Medal in Anatomy, Physiology and Chemistry and in 1883 had received the silver medal in Forensic Medicine and Toxicology, Pathology and Morbid Anatomy. This alone would not have impressed them enough to allow the erection of the monument but they did want the money being offered in the form of the scholarship and, realising that Eliza was a woman whose wishes were not easily thwarted, they reluctantly agreed.
Eliza began to see the Trustees as her friends and family and would consult them on matters which were not really any concern of theirs.

Details of her promised bequest appeared in newspapers and she was quite surprised when this publicity led to a spate of begging letters. She sought advice from the Royal College of Surgeons on how to deal with these requests.

She now had to turn her attention to the final part of her plan. She needed a sculptor to carry out her wishes and produce the memorial to Mac.

Her younger brother Victor had studied sculpture in Italy and while there had become friendly with Alfred Gilbert. He had told Eliza of the brilliance of this artist whose works included the Statue of Eros in London and more recently the Tomb of the Duke of Clarence. Never one to be satisfied with less than the best, Eliza set off for Bruges to make contact with Gilbert. There is no doubt that Eliza's beauty and her persuasiveness would have played a major role in obtaining Gilbert's acceptance of this commission. His clients included the highest in the land and he certainly did not require a commission of this kind in order to enhance his reputation. Together they drew up the plans for the monument which she then took back to the Royal College of Surgeons for their approval. They had been prepared to accept what they assumed would be a small, discreet memorial to Mac. They were not prepared for what she showed them in the plans. The monument would be a five feet high bronze and marble pedestal with decoration which would be a memorial not only to Mac but to his philosophies and their lives together.

The Trustees had not expected though that on top of the pedestal would be a casket containing Mac's ashes. The casket would have a lock with two keys. On her death, the casket was to be opened and her ashes mingled with Mac's – for eternity. A further surprise came when they discovered that the two bronze heads of Mac and Eliza would rest above the casket. The Trustees had not wanted the memorial but they did want the scholarship and if that meant they had to accept not only Mac but also Eliza, then so be it. They were also delighted to accept her gift of the marble floor upon which the monument would rest, with her signature in the marble tile to the right of the monument.

Eliza was now to discover that she was destined to join a queue of people awaiting completion of their works by Gilbert and so to encourage him to finish the product quickly she barely left him alone. Eliza became totally absorbed in this work and encouraged Gilbert at every stage. In order that he should fully appreciate her gratitude she

123

sought a way of repaying him. Eliza loved giving to others but she almost demanded that her gifts were truly appreciated. She could become either depressed or angry according to her mood if she felt that someone who had been chosen by her to receive a gift, however small, was not suitably grateful for it. She had long since ceased giving presents to her brothers because her choice had not always been to their taste and so they had not been truly appreciative.

Now she sought to reward Gilbert in the best possible way. He was to be well paid for his work but that was not enough for Eliza. She showered him with gifts and letters. She stayed with him, supporting and encouraging him every step of the way. Although this work was a tribute to the love she and the doctor had for each other, she now devoted herself to Gilbert. Together they planned a more permanent tribute to the relationship that was growing between them. As the heads of the two figures were nearing completion, she persuaded Gilbert to make a small recess in the top of her head. There was to be a hinged lid covering it and it would be used to house some of Gilbert's ashes upon his death. Eliza could see no disloyalty to Mac in this proposal, only a tribute to Gilbert who had been the means through which they could be reunited in death. Surely, she thought, there could be no greater tribute than this.

Eliza found in Gilbert and his mother soulmates who could sympathise with her artistic temperament without seeing it as some kind of madness which was how many people seemed to view it. His mother was initially grateful that Eliza seemed to have a sufficiently beneficial influence on Alfred to keep him working consistently for once. Other members of his circle were also aware of the influence she had upon him.

As well as the heads of Eliza and Mac for the memorial, Gilbert also sculpted a bust of Eliza, entitled Eheu Fugaces. Marian Spielman of the Magazine of Arts wrote some lines of verse to accompany this work as was often the practice at that time.

The lines read:

Enchantress of a Genius

Victor of a Heart

Laughing lips and bright compelling eyes that whip

Into a great dull'd soul, awakening at the dart, Zeal, Hope and Poetry

Once again impart a power that fast was fading from his loosening grip.

Mark how a sweet-willed woman, passionate for Art-

A passion exquisite and deep

A love sublime

Called forth responding passion on the Artist's part

Lifting him back to heights he would no longer climb!

Oh take our thanks! Oh take our love for such a deed.

Great the fair service done in his hour of need.

He found a friend to help him serve his magic hand,

Leading to the clay that quickens at his touch.

Inspired with life immortal.

Could we overmuch, Nay - could we laud enough the triumph

The Command.

Spielmann was embarrassed when some people interpreted these lines as being a declaration of his own love for Eliza when he had intended them only as gratitude for the influence she was having on Gilbert's work.

Eliza, in turn, asked Gilbert to sit for a professional photographer friend of hers. The resulting portrait was later presented to Eliza with the inscription, 'For Ever, forever'. There was no doubt that Eliza found in Gilbert someone who could fill the void left by Mac. Never could anyone replace him but she needed to love and be loved in return. For a while she was happier than she had been since Mac's death. It was not to last.

The completed memorial was to be entitled 'Mors, Janua Vitae' - Death the Doorway to Life. Once the work was completed in its plaster form, it was exhibited at the Royal Academy in 1907. Gilbert consulted Eliza before agreeing to the exhibition and they agreed it would be better if no mention was made of the identities of the two heads or of the purpose of the memorial. However it would be exhibited under its intended title, Mors Janua Vitae.

Eliza was fully in agreement with this arrangement and the work was duly exhibited. However, alone once more, Eliza began to think that there would be greater public interest in the work if the world were to know its true purpose. She wrote to Marian Spielmann and told him the whole story.

When she told Gilbert, somewhat reluctantly, of her actions, he was furious. He wrote to Spielmann begging him to regard whatever she had said as totally unauthorised and irresponsible. Gilbert was disappointed in Eliza. He thought their relationship was founded on trust and he now felt unable to trust her.

Without her to spur him on, he felt unable to finish the project. Eliza tried every means at her disposal to get him to complete it and then when these failed, she tried to get it from him in its unfinished state.

Eliza was becoming increasingly frustrated with Gilbert. She was trying to oversee the completion of the memorial while at the same time maintaining her house in Southport. The strain of all the travelling was beginning to tell upon her. She decided reluctantly that she had no alternative but to sell the wonderful house in Southport, put most of her furniture in store and move down to London. There at least she would be within easy reach of the Royal College of Surgeons and her other contacts.

While Mac had been able to anticipate her rages, Gilbert was unprepared for them. In one rage she smashed the windows of his studio with stones and conducted such a tirade of abuse against him that he was forced to hand over the memorial. Gilbert, it seemed, was deeply hurt by Eliza's actions. He had found her a fascinating woman who had supported him at a time when he needed it most. Their relationship was now forced to end.

When finally Eliza took charge of the memorial and the plaster head which Gilbert had made of her, she needed to find someone to finish them. She turned to Albert Toft. He arranged for the two items to be cast in bronze by a highly reputable company in Germany. So delighted was Eliza with the help he had given her that she hoped he would do further work for her. He however was not to be beguiled by her as Gilbert had been and once he saw that her temper was becoming aroused, he sent back her cheque and declined the commission.

Eliza was beginning to earn for herself the reputation of a dangerous and unpredictable woman. She was desperate for friendship and love and often thought that by lavishing gifts upon people she would buy their love and affection. The friends she had were often subjected to abuse in her moments of rage and so deserted her out of desire for self-preservation.

She would invite guests to her house for dinner, with excellent food and fine wines, but if the conversation turned to some subject about which Eliza felt strongly, she would become more and more irate. All attempts to console her by changing the subject would fail and the evening often ended with Eliza ordering the guests out of the house or in her beginning to damage the furniture in her rage. Such occasions were embarrassing and even her closest friends found it difficult to remain so after several such encounters.

Although Gilbert had gone from Eliza's life, he was still very much in the public eye. His reputation for being unable to complete commissions had led to the Royal Academy demanding his resignation. Both Gilbert and his mother sent beseeching requests to the King, who as Patron of the Royal Academy was the only person able to expel a member. Unknown to them, Eliza, having heard of his plight, sent a letter to the King extolling his genius and begging him to repeal the expulsion.

127

Unfortunately, her handwriting bore such a close resemblance to that of Gilbert, that it was believed Gilbert had written the letter himself on his own behalf. Less than a month later, Alfred Gilbert accepted that he had no alternative but to voluntarily resign his membership.

In April 1909, exactly five years after Mac's death, the Monument was erected in the lobby of the Royal College of Surgeons, where, in accordance with Eliza's conditions, it should remain undisturbed for ever. The marble tile to the right of the monument bore her signature. Eliza hoped that everyone who ever visited the Royal College of Surgeons from that day would see it and be told of its significance.

Eliza had spent some considerable time and expense in choosing the right spot, immediately to the left of the entrance, and in ensuring that the surroundings were the perfect resting place for her lover. She chose the finest marble for the floor, negotiating upon the necessary thickness, and from this was laid the Entrance Hall, the Museum vestibule, the Main Hall and the corridor. The total cost was over £600.

These five years had been busy and demanding for Eliza. Much of the time had been spent travelling backwards and forwards between England and Belgium in order to keep Gilbert engaged in his work. Not only this, but she had spent a large amount of time in Southport, sorting through Mac's belongings, particularly his writings. Now she gathered them together in some sort of order so that they presented a chronological account of his theories. There was also a report of their court case in Southport, aptly titled 'The Woman Who Did'.

These alone were not enough as she needed to explain who he was and draw them all together into a coherent whole. She began writing an introduction, describing his birth and progression into the medical profession. She described their meeting, their love-marriage and finally their separation. Once it was all assembled she tried to find someone to publish it in book form. It was entitled 'Deliberate Writings'- a tribute to his memory. The inside of the cover was decorated with his monogram and everywhere there were pink roses.

Inside was printed a letter
'My dear ...
May I invite your acceptance of a book to interest you I hope, whether or not you are in sympathy with Atheists. Be generous! Experience rapture. It is for me to cause to be remembered a Surgeon whose whole life- as long as he was fit - was devoted to useful, good work. After he was fit, for he was fully conscious and able to hearken to the needs of sufferers, and think what could be done for their sakes and prescribe for them in writing,- and when speech left him, he stood waiting and ready for Death. A life of 'Virtue be thou my God' nor spot, nor soil; without blemish. I would I knew how to describe him to you.
Faithfully,'

Eliza determined that Mac would never be forgotten.
She sent copies of this privately printed book to all her brothers so that they would at last know what a wonderful man he had been and why she had forsaken her family in order to devote her life to him.

Eliza also sent copies of the book and of a collection of poetry to the Royal College of Surgeons where they were kept safely along with other documents appertaining to this remarkable chapter in its history.

Eliza never forgot Alfred Gilbert, although it seems he did try to forget her. Disgraced as he had been in the eyes of the Art World, he could have done well to seek solace from the friendship Eliza was offering him. However his family and immediate circle of friends successfully persuaded him that Eliza was insane. For the good of whatever reputation he still had, he was advised to steer clear of her.

The treatment she received from these people hurt Eliza more than anyone realised. She was alone once more in a cruel world dominated, she maintained, by men and their opinions.

Elated that the Memorial was now finally in place, Eliza felt she wanted the whole world to know about it. She decided she must now find a permanent place to live and she chose a flat in Maida Vale. The building was elegant and the street quiet, although there were a few shops within walking distance. Once she had moved her furniture and other belongings in there she felt that now she was ready to get on with her life. She remembered the day she had moved into her little house in Wigan and the day she and Mac had moved into the wonderful house in Southport. One one thing marred her joy on this day. Mac was not there to share it with her.

The Trustees of the Royal College of Surgeons now wanted some tangible evidence of Eliza's intention of bequeathing a scholarship in Mac's memory. They insisted that she made a Will in which they would be the main beneficiary of her fortune. Until now she had made verbal and written offers and they had accepted the memorial in anticipation of greater things to come. Eliza's family knew very little other than that she had erected the memorial in Mac's honour.

She was aware that she had neglected her family over the past five years and she decided to make amends for this. She decided to go back to Southport for a few days, contact her Solicitor about the drawing up of the Will and visit her family.

While she was there she found time to reply to the many letters she had received and which so far remained unanswered. Some two years previously her dearest brother Edward had married his childhood sweetheart Nellie and they had gone off to the other side of the world to set up home in New Zealand. Her heart would have broken at his departure had she not been totally consumed by her own personal grief.

He had written to her often and told her all his news. Now she had received a letter telling her of the birth of their first child, a little girl born on January 1st. He had enclosed photographs of himself and his wife and baby and Eliza was delighted to see them looking so happy. Now that she had time, she sat down and wrote to Edward, telling him how beautiful she thought his wife and baby were, enquiring after the name of the child and suggesting to him that if he let her know the exact time of the baby's birth she would request the Astrologer Royal to prepare a personal horoscope for the child.

She and Mac had always treated the stars with respect. If they had to believe in a power, other than a God, then the stars would be that power.

This done she contacted her solicitor. Mr Heald had been more than just a solicitor; he had been a family and personal friend. She would always turn to him for advice whenever she needed it and now was such a time. She outlined to him her plans to bequeath the scholarship to the Royal College of Surgeons. This would form the basis of a Trust Fund, the interest from which would be used to provide five scholarships for young men hoping to qualify as Surgeons. Mr Heald hesitated before he answered her.

"Eliza, I implore you to think again about bequeathing such a large amount of money to these people. They are nothing to you. What about your own family: your parents and your brothers and sisters? Surely they deserve to be cared for more than the Royal College of Surgeons who already have a great deal of wealth?"

Eliza felt the anger rising within her again and thought of how Mac always helped her to control these rages.

"My family almost disowned me when I went to live with the doctor" she reminded him. "They have never approved of anything I have done, so why should they think they have a right to the doctor's money, because that is what it is. I wouldn't have a penny if he had not left this to me."

"That is as it may be, but I still think you should ensure that they are provided for if you possibly can. The Royal College of Surgeons doesn't care two snaps for you. Why don't you spend all your money on yourself, both capital and interest. If you do leave anything, leave it to those who have done you good turns."

"I have every intention of providing for my mother and my sisters, I feel that they are the victims of circumstance and need to be looked after. My father always thought of himself first and he can continue to do that. As for my brothers, they are men and can always provide for themselves."

Mr Heald knew that there was truth in what she said but he had to consider his reputation in the town. There was bound to be an outcry when the details of Eliza's Will became known and he might be seen as being a party to this. He chose his words carefully.

"I think you might be wiser to secure the services of a London Solicitor to deal with this matter. After all, that is where you now reside. If I can do anything at all to help you, I always will but as for drawing up this Will, I think this is a matter for somebody else. I will give you the address of my brother Frederic who has chambers in Argyle Place, just off Regent Street. He will be only too pleased to be of service to you and he will be more easily accessible to you."

He wrote down the details of his brother's rooms and handed it to Eliza. She was angry and hurt but she carefully folded the piece of paper and put it into her bag, not knowing whether or not she would ever need to use it.

CHAPTER 7

She worked out in her mind where her priorities lay.
The most important thing that should happen upon her death was that
her remains should be reunited with those of her doctor.

Her Will read:

*After my death, my body shall be enclosed in a plain wooden coffin,
covered smoothly with plain white cloth, without any metal furniture
except (if necessary) a bronze handle at the head and foot.*

*My body is not to be clad in an ordinary shroud but is to be completely
veiled with the white silk crepe veil which I have for the purpose and
which will be found in the casket which I keep by me for the purpose of
holding my ashes after the cremation of my body. No nameplate is to be
affixed to my coffin but my visiting card is to be used for that purpose
instead. Like my late husband, I desire that my body shall subsequently
be cremated and without any religious ceremony in the presence of my
Executor and Trustee or his representative and such persons as may be
required by Law and the regulations of the crematorium and I further
direct that after the cremation of my remains my ashes shall be placed
in the aforesaid casket which I keep by me for the purpose and shall then
be conveyed to the Royal College of Surgeons where they are to be
allowed to mingle with those of my late husband contained in the
Bronze Casket of "Mors Janua Vitae" the work of Alfred Gilbert, MVO
RA, erected there and for this purpose I request the President and
Council of the said College to allow the said casket to be opened. There
are two keys for this purpose, one of which will be found with my Will
and the other is in the keeping of the Secretary of the said College. After*

the casket has been unlocked, the lid can be drawn off, when the cinerary urn will be exposed to view. The lid of this unscrews. After my ashes are in the urn with those of my late husband, the cover to the urn is then to be screwed down again and the lid replaced on the casket which is to be closed and locked for all future time. The two keys are then to be forthwith destroyed. The date of my death should then be engraved on the pedestal.

Eliza's next concern was for her mother. Susannah had never had any money of her own and Eliza intended to rectify this. An annuity of one hundred pounds a year was to be paid to Susannah in equal half-yearly instalments, commencing six months after Eliza's death. Upon her mother's death this was to be paid to her father.

She wanted to remember her two sisters and to ensure that they also had something of their own. To Margaret she bequeathed one hundred pounds, her piano and all her furniture, pictures, prints, ornaments and contents of her Drawing and Dining Rooms. If Margaret were to predecease her, all of these would be shared equally between Margaret's two children, Beatrice and Alex.

To her sister Beatrice she bequeathed one hundred pounds and all the rest of her furniture, her watches, trinkets, jewellery and clothes. In the event that Beatrice should predecease her, these were to be added to Margaret's bequests.

She decreed that all her bronzes and busts not otherwise bequeathed, together with all her other treasures were to be offered at auction.

Once she had made suitable provision for her own family she turned her attention to the Royal College of Surgeons.

Five scholarships were to be founded in the first year and another in each of the next four subsequent years. The exact sum would depend upon the amount of interest earned by the initial investment. The scholarships were to be called the" 'Macloghlin scholarships' founded by Mrs Macloghlin in memory of her husband the late Edward Percy Plantagenet Macloghlin Royal College of Surgeons formerly of Wigan"

The conditions upon which depended the awarding of the scholarships were specifically laid down. The Will was witnessed by Henry Morris, the surgeon who had been such a stalwart friend and supporter of Eliza and Mac and by the Solicitor who drew up the Will.

This done, Eliza felt she could get on with living her life. She wrote many letters to her friends and family. This was one of her dearest occupations, writing letters. Her handwriting was at times barely legible but she made the excuse that her heart had so much to tell that her hand could not keep up the pace. She prepared herself for lengthy handwriting sessions, with paper, envelopes and ink at the ready. She would then take out one of her most treasured possessions, the old pen that Alfred Gilbert had given her during the period of their relationship. She had asked that after her death, that too should be offered at auction.

She wrote often to her brother Edward in New Zealand, sharing his joy at the births of each of his children. She lavished gifts upon each one of them in turn and gained the sort of pleasure she imagined she would have gained from having her own children. These thoughts usually reduced Eliza to tears as she remembered the trauma of discovering that she would never experience the joys of motherhood. She had trusted Mac then as always. He must be right, he must know best. But did he?

The periods of joy and enthusiasm for life were few and far between now. She more often felt consumed by bitterness at the way life had treated her. She had done what she had wanted to do, she realised that, but having remained loyal to one man for most of her life she had been castigated by society and scorned by her own family. The doctor had not had to suffer to the same extent. His professional competence had been sufficient for most people; his private life appeared to be of little importance.

On the whole it seemed to Eliza once more that there was one code of ethics to which women must adhere and a totally different one for men. She began to hate and distrust men completely. This was a world totally ruled by men for their own benefits. She had tremendous sympathy with the Suffragette movement of which many of her friends were members. She wondered whether one day women would be able to stand equally beside men in this world.

The year passed and the next and then shortly before Christmas of 1911 she decided to invite her sister Margaret to stay with her while Harold, her husband, was working overseas. Her sister would dearly have loved to join him in Singapore but she needed to be at home with the children.

Margaret seized the opportunity to go down to London on the train to stay with Eliza. She and the two children were on a train as soon as she could make the arrangements. The children could only stay for a few days as they had to return to go back to school and Margaret was sad to see them leave with Margaret's housekeeper who had arrived to escort them back.

The two sisters enjoyed each other's company and it was wonderful for Eliza to have someone to talk to and to go on shopping trips with. She loved to buy things for Margaret and the children. It was a time of great happiness for them both.

While they were together, Eliza decided that she must confide in Margaret about the contents of her Will and her plans for the Macloghlin Scholarship. She expected Margaret to be as excited about it as she was and to be pleased to hear that she was going to benefit so generously from the Will. Eliza told her about the plans. Margaret listened but, with her hands twisting nervously around each other, she tried to find the right words to say.

"But Eliza, what about your family? Don't you think we are more deserving than the Royal College of Surgeons?"

Eliza could barely believe her ears. She had provided most generously for her parents and her sisters. They had given her nothing and had wanted to know nothing about her once she had gone to live with Mac, but now they 'deserved' his money. Eliza was furious. She flew into an uncontrollable rage which terrified Margaret. Rushing into the bedroom, Margaret sat on the bed, sobbing. She had never seen Eliza like this. She did not know how to deal with the situation. A nervous woman at the best of times, this was more than she could bear. She was grateful that the children had not seen this outburst. For the first time since they had left, she was glad they were now safely back home.

Suddenly the door burst open and Eliza stood there, her face contorted with anger. "Get out of my house this moment, you ungrateful woman!" she screamed. Margaret began to throw her belongings into a bag. She couldn't wait to get away from this woman whom she thought she knew but who was now behaving in this insane, irrational manner. She rushed out into the street with her bag and hailed a taxi cab, something she had never needed to do in her life up until this moment. She had no idea where she was going and told the driver the only place she could think of. "Euston Station please"

The next few hours were something of a nightmare for Margaret. She arrived at the station only to find that there were no more trains that day. She went into the refreshment room and sat at an empty table. She was conscious of the stares of the people around her. She must have looked an odd sight. She had thrown on a coat and had hardly combed her hair. Here she was, sitting forlornly facing a cup of tea which was rapidly going cold.

At last she became calmer and decided that, terrified though she was, she could not desert Eliza now. Her sister was obviously sick and needed help and comfort. She had seen similar signs in her own husband on occasions and knew how important it was for him to have her support at such times. Picking up her bag, she left the refreshment room and ventured out into the street. She decided not to take another taxi which would be extravagant, but to take the bus. The journey would take longer and that would give her more time to sort out her feelings before arriving back at Maida Vale.

Eliza had watched her go without really understanding what was happening.

She felt calmer now and wished she had not driven her sister away, but her word still rang in her ears. "Deserving" deserving indeed!

She lay on her couch and slept fitfully. She was aroused by the ringing of the front door bell. The maid opened the door and was amazed to see a dishevelled Margaret standing there, bag in hand. Eliza hugged her sister and apologised sincerely for the treatment she had meted out to her. The two wept with relief that they were together again and the ordeal was over. Margaret suggested that Eliza should consult a doctor about her depression and bouts of anger and Eliza agreed.

Mr. F. W. Price of Harley St was called and arrived at the flat the next day. After a brief examination he diagnosed that she had an enlarged heart and prescribed some medication which might help the condition. He insisted there was nothing to worry about as it was simply caused by the pressure she had been under for so long. He was sure that once she was rested, the symptoms would disappear and her mood would improve accordingly.

Eliza took the tablets prescribed and found she was sleeping much better. She was happy that now she was resting she would become happier and less tense. Meanwhile, Margaret had not managed to put the question of the Will out of her mind. She dared not raise the subject again for fear of a recurrence of a similar response and so she decided

138

to write to her father, explaining the situation to him and asking for his advice. She received a reply within a few days which indicated to her that her family considered the matter important. However, the reply was not from her father but from her brother George. It was carefully worded so that if by chance Eliza should read it, she wouldn't realise that Margaret had told them about the Will.

My dear Sister

Thank you for keeping us informed about yourself and your sister. We are grateful that you gave us the information you did. Father and I have discussed the matter and think it would be advisable for the matter of priorities could be settled. We have always respected Eliza's wish to live her own life as she chose to do and we hope she appreciates that after all, we are her flesh and blood and will always support her whatever happens. We are glad that she has consulted a doctor about her problems and perhaps he might be able to help in proving that her illness has made her act a little rashly at times.

Our love to you all as ever
Your loving brother George.

Margaret carefully stored the letter away. Ambiguous though it might appear, she was sure that Eliza would see through it immediately.

One evening, Margaret could wait no longer
"Eliza, I have been thinking about your Will. I know you became angry with me last time I spoke about it but there is one thing that worries me. Just supposing that during your lifetime you spend almost all of the money you have. There may not be enough left to give the scholarship and all the other sums of money as well"

Eliza considered this and then quite calmly replied
"I am aware of that. I may live for quite a long time or I may not. We cannot know such things. So I must be very thrifty with my money. I shall make my own clothes and I shall just have the one maidservant.

That way I shall spend as little as possible and there will be plenty left for all the things I have stated in my Will."

Margaret could not leave it there, however. Now that she had the support of her father and brother she had the courage to pursue the matter.

"What a pity to have to live so frugally, just so that there will be enough left for us" she said

Eliza was not stupid. She knew what Margaret was trying to do.

"It is not you I am concerned about, Margaret. It is my scholarship to the Royal College of Surgeons that matters. That must be paid at all costs, even if it means there isn't anything left for the other legacies"

Margaret realised that this was what George meant in his letter. She had to settle the 'matter of priorities'

"I am not thinking of myself, Eliza, but of our poor mother. If there is only enough left for the scholarship then it seems she might get nothing.

Margaret tried to appear distraught at the thought of her 'poor mother' but Eliza was not fooled. She thought hard and then, crossing over to her desk, she took out the papers. She read for some time before speaking,
"Margaret, you were quite right to bring this to my attention. I have stipulated that the scholarship must be paid in preference to all other payments which would mean that if there is only ten thousand pounds left then you and my parents would receive nothing. If I reversed these priorities so that my scholarship can only be paid after all the other legacies have been allocated, would that satisfy you?"

This seemed most acceptable to Margaret and hoped her brother and father would agree. So she wrote to inform them.

To Eliza, this small change in priorities meant little. She had already decided that come what may, there would always be sufficient funds to provide for her family and the scholarship. If she could please Margaret by making this alteration then so be it.

The tablets prescribed for her were now beginning to have a strange effect on her. She became light headed and was sometimes unaware that people were talking to her. She was often sick after her meals and was rapidly losing weight. It was because of these unpleasant side-effects that she asked the doctors to visit her. Her doctor Dr. F W Price was due to visit her the following day and he was to be accompanied by his partner, Dr Mackenzie. Eliza thought that this would be an ideal opportunity to draw up a Codicil to her Will and ask two such respected gentlemen to witness it.

Early next morning she took out Alfred Gilbert's old pen and sat down at her writing desk.

This is a Codicil to the Last Will and Testament of me, Eliza Macloghlin........

..............whereas by my said Will I directed that the legacy of ten thousand pounds free from duty to the Royal College of Surgeons together with the duty thereon be paid in priority to any other legacies bequeathed.........I now hereby revoke such direction and direct that the annuity given to my mother and the annuity given to my father after the death of my mother....and all pecuniary and specific legacies given to my sister Margaret and her children and my sister Beatrice Millard shall be paid over in priority to the aforesaid legacy or sum of ten thousand pounds. In all other respects I confirm my said Will....

Eliza read it carefully to herself and then out loud to Margaret.
" Does that seem to make things more acceptable?" She asked

Her sister was embarrassed by the situation but she nodded her agreement.

When the doctors arrived, Eliza asked them to read what she had written and to witness her signature and to add their own.

They were aware of Margaret hovering in the background and after all had been completed they took her to one side and asked how Eliza had appeared and whether the question of the Will had possibly been causing her anxiety and distress.

"She has not been well since you gave her those tablets. She has not been herself at all. I think she realised that she would need her family to support her and ought to ensure that they were cared for in her Will"

"I am going to increase the dosage of her medication" The Doctor decided, "Will you ensure that she takes them regularly?"

Margaret agreed. Always happy to be able to do something useful for Eliza.

The two doctors left and Eliza appeared to be satisfied with her morning's work. Soon after this, Margaret received a letter which stunned them all. Her husband had been admitted to an institution in Singapore - apparently so that his condition could be investigated more thoroughly.

Eliza dreaded being alone and hoped that this news would not mean Margaret leaving to be with him. As this anxiety increased, Dr Price prescribed larger and larger doses of the medication.
Meanwhile, Eliza was constantly in touch with her brother Edward in New Zealand. He kept her informed about his family life. After the birth of their first child, Nellie, the couple had returned to England. They had packed all their belongings into shipping crates and undertaken the long

sea voyage with the young baby. However, life was not as sweet as they had anticipated. His father had retired and his brother Alfred was now in charge of the studio. The two brothers were not the best of friends and Edward found it impossible to work with him. Nellie, Edward's wife was given a job as housekeeper in Alfred's house in return for receiving a roof over their heads. The situation was intolerable and they very quickly repacked their belongings and returned to the other side of the world. Eliza had never had the chance to say Goodbye to them and had no idea why they had gone. She wondered whether she could have done more to help. Were they so poor that they could not afford to live her any longer? Surely the fare back to New Zealand must have cost a fortune.

Eliza resented the fact that she had so much money and they had none and yet Edward appeared too proud to ask for help.

In her next letter she asked him all these things but he carefully avoided the issue in his letters. He had experienced enough of the bigotry within his family and he did not want to be accused of currying favour with his sister. Concerned that he might indeed be poor or even destitute out in the wilds of New Zealand where he had set up his studio, Eliza came up with a plan which would help his children thrive. She went out and bought one dozen jars of Horlicks Malted Milk at a cost of eleven shillings a jar. Surely this was something he could never afford himself and it would do the children so much good. She had them carefully packed by the shop and they were duly despatched to Edward.
When they arrived, he was amazed to receive such a gift and immediately hit on the idea of taking a photograph of the children which incorporated the jar of Horlicks.

It showed the two children sitting on either side of the jar. John was smiling sweetly and holding an empty cup, while Nellie stirred the drink. He knew Eliza would be thrilled with the picture but could never have predicted just how thrilled she would be.

When Eliza opened the package and saw the picture she wanted to run into the street and show everyone in London. She thought of a way of showing it to more and more people and helping Edward and his family at the same time. She had the picture enlarged and sent it to the manufacturers of Horlicks with a letter suggesting that they might use it to advertise their product. Her pen as usual flowed flamboyantly as she praised her brother and the beauty of his children. She was in no doubt that Horlicks Malted Milk Company would seize the opportunity to benefit from this wonderful advertising feature. She warned them however, that they must not use it at all, nor use any of her words of recommendation unless they were prepared to pay a substantial sum of money towards the educations of Nellie and John.

Eliza wondered how the letter would be received. She had nothing to lose, she would either receive the picture back or her brother's children would financially be considerably better off.

However she was both disappointed and angry when she received a reply to her letter two days later. They were pleased that she regarded their product so highly but were not in the habit of using photographs in that way. If they were to respond to every plea for gratuitous gifts they would indeed soon be bankrupt. Did she realise how difficult it was to make the books balance at the end of the year? However, they had decided to send six eleven shilling jars of Horlicks to New Zealand to Edward.

Eliza was scathing in her reply. Her tongue and her pen could be caustic at times and this was such a time. She reminded them that she had sent jars of Virol out to New Zealand also and intimated that that company might benefit from her generosity. However she thanked them for their actions returned to them the picture for their records and again asked that they did not use it for any purpose without her express permission.

She began to feel a great sense of responsibility towards her brother and his children. She also felt similarly towards Margaret and her children. They would be the ones to follow and deserved her help.

The tablets she was still taking were making her feel worse by the hour. Some days she couldn't get out of bed and she could barely eat, such was the intensity of the nausea.

She went to the bookcase and took down one of Mac's medical textbooks. She searched for something which might give her an idea of why she felt so ill. As she had suspected, the tablets were indeed Digitalis. She read about their effects in the book and they matched her own symptoms exactly. These, though, were the effects of too large a dose. In smaller quantities they would have been quite an effective remedy for her heart defects. She began to suspect that the doctor was trying to poison her!

Lying in bed almost delirious and barely conscious at times, she remembered the day when Margaret had been talking to the two doctors after they had witnessed the Codicil to her will. It was after that that the dosage had been increased. Margaret must have persuaded them to do something to shorten her life so that here would be more money for her to receive when the time came. She did not want to believe that her sister could do such a thing.

Eliza was becoming very erratic in her moods. She was forgetful and sometimes could not remember the gist of a sentence long enough to get to the end of it. Added to this she was becoming aware of a deficiency in her hearing. That was something she tried to hide at all costs.

Her conviction that Margaret was in league with the doctors in trying to poison her strengthened.

Eliza told her with some difficulty that she was going to write another Codicil to the will. This time the legacy of one hundred pounds, which she had left to Margaret, was to be replaced by an annuity of one hundred and fifty pounds per year until her children reached the age of twenty-one. In this way Margaret would have a small income of her own to enable her to educate her children. In the event of Margaret herself dying before they reached that age, they would each get seventy-five pounds annually.

Surely, Eliza thought, when she realised how generous I am being towards her she will not allow me to be poisoned in this way.

Eliza was desperate for help. Help from someone she could trust. But who? The solicitors thought that she was wrong in leaving her money in this way, the doctors were poisoning her and her sister was assisting them to do so. Then she decided to go to see the only person she could trust and who would listen to her without assuming her to be mad – Rickman J Godlee the President of the Royal College of Surgeons. His home was in Wimpole Street and it was there that she went with Margaret on the afternoon of the seventh of April 1913. Dr Godlee was amazed to see her but knew that this woman was too valuable to dismiss. He agreed to witness and sign this new Codicil along with his parlourmaid who happened to be the only other person present in the house at the time.

As they returned home, Eliza was looking over her shoulder all the time, convinced she was being followed. Margaret was frightened by the state in which she found Eliza but dismissed ideas that the doctors might have been wrong in prescribing those particular tablets. Surely doctors would know what they were doing.

The days that followed were unbearable for Margaret and Eliza. Each felt helpless and alone. Eliza begged Margaret to summon a different doctor so that he might examine her and prove that the others had been wrong but Margaret was unwilling to do this. Eliza eventually persuaded Margaret to contact Rickman Godlee and ask him to visit her at the same time as Dr F W Price. Margaret was sure this could do no harm and the two men were summoned. On their arrival they were shown into the drawing room. Eliza was feeling much better that day but did not want to give the impression that she had invented her previous symptoms. She walked slowly into the room, supported by a walking stick. The two men stood up as she entered. Signalling to them to sit, she moved over to the chaise longue and carefully arranged herself upon it. Margaret sat opposite to her. The two men were unsure why they had been summoned and while tea was being served they tried to make polite conversation.

'How do you like living in London, Mrs Street?' they asked of Margaret. 'I expect you envy your sister the kind of lifestyle she enjoys'
'Margaret has no need to be envious of me at all' interrupted Eliza, 'I look after her very well and make sure that she wants for nothing. Once I am gone she will be quite well provided for I can assure you'.

Eliza did not now appear to be such a sick woman and Margaret wondered how she had made such a rapid recovery. As she saw the two doctors out into the hall, Margaret whispered to Dr Price, 'She thinks you are trying to poison her.'

Dr Price stood still and stared at Margaret.
"Trying to poison her? What on earth can you mean?"
"The tablets have made her ill and when she read about them in a medical book she found that they were poisonous if taken in large quantities"'.
"But she looks quite well today" exclaimed the doctor.
"That is because she has taken no tablets, she is afraid of you"
Dr Price was angry but at the same time worried for his own reputation.

Admittedly he had prescribed a relatively large dose but he was confident that it would not be so great as to poison her. He hoped this story did not get passed around.

"Listen Mrs Street; please do not tell a soul about this. It seems that she is becoming mentally unbalanced and we would not like that to become widely known would we?"

Margaret was horrified at this suggestion but realised that it would be a satisfactory explanation for many of Eliza's actions.

CHAPTER 8

Margaret and her children stayed with Eliza for the next six weeks during which time Eliza barely moved from her bed. She would plead with Margaret to help her as she was near to death. Sometimes when she did feel able to leave her bed she would behave in a most irrational manner. On one occasion Margaret caught her about to leave the house in her undergarments. She persuaded her to return indoors and put on some more clothes while the weather was still a little chilly for May. Margaret found it difficult to keep the knowledge of Eliza's condition from the children and she did not want them to become distressed by what they might see.

Then just as life was becoming very difficult indeed for Margaret, Eliza would appear perfectly normal again and Margaret would hope that things were getting better. The two sisters would talk about their days as girls in Wigan and about their brothers and sister Beatrice. Those had been happy days and Margaret hoped that talking about them would help to calm Eliza down. However, one night as Eliza was talking about her father, she became quite agitated.

"I do not trust that man" she said, "he has made life very difficult for Mother. She loves him dearly I am sure, but she is so afraid of upsetting him that she has never been able to have a life of her own. I have made sure that if she should die first, the annuity of one hundred pounds a year would go to him but I am beginning to think that is too much for him. He might meet another woman who would look after him in his old age and then my money would go to her. He might decide to go to New Zealand and disrupt Edward and Victor's lives. No, I must put a stop to that at once."

Margaret was desperate. Surely there had been enough trouble already regarding this Will. She just wanted a peaceful life.

However, once Eliza's mind was made up, nothing would change it.

The following day Eliza sent for Frederic Heald to visit her at the flat.

He wondered just how long this matter would continue before something happened one way or another. He felt he had a duty to his brother and to Eliza's father who was in constant touch with him and yet he really did not want to add to this lady's unhappiness.

On the 28th May 1913, while life in London was attempting to carry on as if the threat of war in Europe did not exist, Mr. Frederic Heald walked up to the front door of Ashworth Mansions and rang the bell of number 40. Hannah Taylor, Eliza's housekeeper opened the door and led him into the drawing room. Eliza looked up as he entered. She looked ill and tired. He had never seen her looking quite so drawn before, even during her period of mourning for her husband. The doctors must know what they are doing, he thought, but whatever that is it does not seem to be doing her much good. Perhaps she is beyond help.

"How are you feeling today? Eliza?" he asked tentatively.

"I think the end is near, my dear Frederic" she smiled weakly.
"That is why I have had some more thoughts regarding my Will; I need to add another Codicil to it".

Frederic Heald sighed inwardly. The second Codicil had been carefully worded to satisfy the needs of her family, he had made sure of that. What changes could she want to make this time?

"I have decided that I cannot give my father so much of my money. I think he has had quite enough of my life already. Will you please write it down for me as I dictate?"

Frederic Heald thought quickly. He did not know what she was going to put in this Codicil but he certainly did not want to be responsible for the wording of it.

"No Eliza, I think it would be better if you wrote it yourself in your own words and then you would be quite sure it was exactly as you want it."

Eliza did not suspect that he had any other reason for not wanting to write it for her and she   went over to her typewriter on her desk and began

'This is the THIRD CODICIL to the last Will and Testament of me ELIZA MACLOGHIN of 40 Ashworth Mansions, Elgin Avenue, Maida Vale in the county of London, Widow, which Will bears the date the twenty second day of April nineteen hundred and ten. WHEREAS by my first Codicil I have given one hundred a year annuity to my Mother for her life and after my said mother's death to my Father for his life INSTEAD I give and bequeath to my Father an annuity of fifty pounds a year free of duty for his life so long as he remains a widower and lives in this country England AND I give the replica of the original bronze bust of me by Alfred Gilbert MVO which said replica is in the wardrobe in my workroom to my sister Margaret Street free of duty And five other replicas to my dear friend Mr Marion Harry Spielmann of 21 Cadogan Gardens to offer the said five replicas to five Art Galleries of the World to be treasured for ever. But the five galleries must pay duty thereon and whichever gallery won't the bronze replica of my bust will not be given to that gallery. Finally I desire my dear friend Mr Marion Harry Spielmann to do his will with the five bronze replicas of my bust by Alfred Gilbert MVO because I know my friend understands me that my bronze bust is a very sacred work indeed. And my sister Margaret Street will give the bronze girl with the hoop in my drawing room to my most trusted friend and solicitor Mr John Heald of Wigan when the whole of my estate is realised and Mr John Heald my most trusted friend has remembered my promise to my husband and my promise to the Royal College of

Surgeons that both promises were and are and forever will be my Vow unto God when I promised my husband and I must pay that vow and when my most trusted friend and Solicitor Mr John C Heald's work is finished for me the best he could do for my Vow unto God Well Done my sister Margaret Street will gladly for my sake give my most trusted friend the bronze girl with the hoop. In all other respects I confirm my said Will except so far as the same is altered by my first Codicil and by my second Codicil both Codicils which I hereby confirm IN WITNESS whereof I have hereunto set my hand this twenty-eighth of May Nineteen hundred and thirteen.

When she had finished writing she handed the paper to the Solicitor to read.

It was a long rambling document written in the kind of language Eliza liked to imagine was poetic.

Mr Heald read it through and then a worried frown creased his face.

"What is the matter?" Eliza asked, knowing full well what the matter was bound to be.

"Your father...." he began

"My father?" Eliza echoed sarcastically. "My father will be furious when he learns about this. But then my father is furious at everything I do or say. There will be nothing new in that". Mr Heald was not in a position to argue with Elisa. He could see problems ahead with this Codicil but she would not listen.

"Would you witness my signature please" she asked "I think my sister Margaret should be called upon to witness it also"

"I beg your indulgence, Eliza but would it not appear a little strange to your father that Margaret had allowed you to add these conditions to your Will? Would it not be better for her if someone else, perhaps Hannah your housekeeper were to sign along with me?"

Eliza decided he was right. As her solicitor he would merely be carrying out her instructions but Margaret would be censured by her father if she were seen to be a party to this.

So Hannah was summoned to the drawing room.

"I would like you and Mr Heald to witness my signature on this paper" she said to the girl.

Eliza took up her pen and signed the Codicil. Then she turned the page over and signed the other page as well.

"There is no need to sign both pages" Mr Heald pointed out.

"I must leave nothing to chance" said Eliza," I must be seen to be thorough unto death".
Mr Heald sighed; he knew that this third Codicil was going to create problems but he had hoped that he could claim that she had written it herself and he had merely witnessed the signature. Now she wanted him to sign both sides indicating his complete participation in the affair.

"This is totally irregular, Mrs Macloghlin" he said irritably.

"Will you sign this now Mr Heald?" Eliza spoke severely as if to a small child. "or do I find a new solicitor for myself?"

Mr Heald almost wished she would do that but he took the pen from Eliza's hand and placed his signature on the pages; Hannah did likewise.

The will was complete and now Eliza felt she could rest.

She took five pound notes from her purse and offered them to Mr Heald. "Here take this for your trouble".

Over the years Eliza had more than paid for the services of both the Heald brothers, both in gifts and money, far over and above their charges, but she still felt bound to offer him something in view of the trouble this signature appeared to have caused him.
"Oh no, I couldn't take anything. After all, I have merely watched you write the Will yourself and added my signature. I have done no more than your housekeeper. Thank you ma'am but I cannot accept payment."

Eliza was touched by his honesty and generosity. She thanked him sincerely and put the money back in her purse.

Frederick Heald offered to see himself out and bade farewell to Eliza. She trusted him – just as she had always trusted the men in her life.

As he stepped out of the drawing room and into the hallway, he caught sight of Margaret, hovering nervously by the stairs.

"Oh, my dear Mrs Street. Eliza has certainly made things difficult again with this new Codicil."
Margaret felt fear such as she had never felt before when she heard these words. "I was afraid she might have something planned and I am sure my father and brothers are going to hold me responsible. After all, they have trusted me to look after their interests."

Frederick looked her straight in the eye and said "I think the time has come when we really are going to have to do something drastic. Eliza is obviously mentally unbalanced and if we can prove this, then the third Codicil at least will have no value."

Margaret's fears increased. Surely he could not be serious. She admitted that her sister did some very strange things but to say she was mentally unbalanced or insane? Those were words she did not want to hear.

Eliza awoke the following morning, happy that she had done all she could to care for her family after her death. In spite of the bitterness she felt towards her father on account of his treatment of both herself and her mother, she knew that she must make provision for both of her parents.

Margaret however had a sleepless night, wondering what was going to happen next. She wanted to please her father and yet felt immense loyalty towards her sister whom she loved dearly. She finally knew what was required. She sent a telegram to her father, telling him briefly that Eliza had done something to her Will that she was sure he would not like.

His reply came later that day. It was brief and to the point.
"Call two doctors and have her committed"

Margaret stared in disbelief at the words which seemed to jump out of the paper and into her very heart. One word in particular – Committed!

It seemed that Margaret was the only person who did not doubt Eliza's sanity and yet she was to be the one to do this dreadful thing to her own sister.

She contacted Dr Price as soon as possible and told him of her father's instruction. He was unhappy about the whole matter but was being paid well by Mrs Street for his care of Eliza.

That night, Dr Price, along with Dr Craig and two nurses drew up in a taxicab outside Eliza's flat. Hannah opened the door as instructed by Margaret but showed them, not into the drawing room, as was usual, but into the kitchen. There Dr Price explained to Margaret and Hannah that they were going to remove Eliza to an asylum for her own safety. Dr Price told Hannah that once Eliza was asleep, they would take over.

Eliza crept into Eliza's room, having expecting to see her asleep she was surprised to see her sitting up in bed reading.

"What is it Hannah? Who is in the kitchen?"
"Some doctors are here ma'am"
"What on earth do you mean? Some doctors!" Eliza was becoming agitated and Hannah feared the worst.
She tried to be calm. "Dr Price and another doctor Ma'am"

Eliza got out of bed, put on her robe and slippers and made her way to the drawing room. She opened the door but found the room empty. In amazement she turned to find Hannah and was in time to see the doctors and nurses creeping into her bedroom.
"What on earth are you doing in my flat?" she called out in panic.
The five conspirators, led by her sister Margaret, swung round in embarrassment. They had no words of explanation, nothing which would provide a satisfactory answer to the unasked questions. Dr Craig was the first to speak.

"I have never met this lady before, but the way in which she is conducting herself this evening does not give me any grounds for considering her to be insane. Just the opposite in fact. I think we all owe her an explanation."

Dr Price tried to talk his way out of this situation but Eliza was not prepared to listen. She ordered them all out of the flat and then she turned to her sister.

Margaret was as white as a sheet, trembling and twisting her handkerchief round and round as she always did in situations like this.

"I cannot begin to understand what you thought you were doing, inviting that horde of strangers into my flat. However, I am warning you now, sister dear, that you must never, no, never, under any circumstances allow them into here again. Do you understand?"

Margaret certainly understood, she stood petrified. But Eliza had not finished with her yet.

"Will you swear on the heads of your two little children that you will never let those...those . persecutors, those so-called doctors into my home again?"

Margaret nodded.

"Nodding your head is no answer" she raged," "Repeat these words after me ----I swear upon the heads of my two little children that I will never again allow those people into this flat"

Margaret repeated the words in a trembling voice, tears pouring relentlessly down her cheeks.

When she returned to the drawing room, she was perturbed to see Eliza burning papers in the fireplace. Eliza laughed as she saw Margaret's worried look.

"Don't worry, sister dear, I am only burning some old papers. I am not burning my Will. There is still going to be plenty for you."

Margaret blushed in embarrassment that Eliza should think about her in that way.

Frederick Heald sat in his chambers with his mind in turmoil. He knew there would be trouble over this Codicil. The wording of it was quite ambiguous and he should never have signed it without making sure that Eliza really understood its implications. Not only had she reduced the amount of money her father would receive, but it could also be construed that her mother should receive nothing.

Pacing the floor of his Chambers, a further thought came to him. He had done this without payment. He had done it as a friend. He had implicated himself still further by so doing. He must rectify this at once.

Taking out his pen he wrote
'Dear Eliza
After further   consideration I have decided to accept your offer of £5. I think you would prefer that our business be conducted in this way

Yours sincerely

Frederick Heald'

Placing the letter in an envelope, he addressed this to Eliza and sent one of his office clerks to deliver it by hand.

Eliza was astounded to receive the letter, but immediately placed a £5 note in an envelope, sealed and addressed it and gave it to the same clerk to return.

Sitting down, she pondered the matter. Why was everyone acting so strangely? Did nobody trust her?

She planned to write to Frederic's brother in Wigan and enclose the letter she had just received. Perhaps he could shed some light on the matter, or at least give her his opinion.

Today she was expecting a visit from Dr Fred Price and from her dear friend Sir Rickman Godlee, the President of the Royal College of Surgeons of England. She had quite deliberately invited them both together. She had tried to explain to Sir Rickman, by letter, just how certain she was that Dr Price was trying to poison her. She thought that if she could see them both together, the matter might be resolved. She knew Sir Rickman would believe her and when he saw that she was receiving incorrect medication for her condition, perhaps such an eminent doctor as he would be able to advise on what she should do about it.

Out of courtesy she had informed each of them that the other would be present. This proved to have been an ill-advised move on Eliza's part for Dr Price immediately suspected that Godlee and Eliza were conspiring against the family in some way. Price decided that the wisest move would be to invite Heald, the Solicitor to be present also.

When her maid announced their arrival, Eliza went into the drawing room and was astonished to find not only the two doctors but also Mr Frederic Heald. She sat down, mentally questioning why he was here. Surely she could not have invited them all here together. She looked directly at Mr Heald and said "You should not be here this morning, our business was completed yesterday. This is a private medical consultation and your presence, for whatever reason, is quite inappropriate. I must ask you to leave"

She summoned her sister and her housekeeper.
"Why is this man here?" she screamed at them. She tried vainly to control the rage she could feel mounting within her – a rage which seemed to render her bereft of any self-control. She had experienced this before and it was unpleasant.

Margaret twisted a handkerchief into knots; she was terrified of Eliza at times like this. Hannah, however, was not terrified of her. In fact she understood fully the pressures upon Eliza. She spoke up in order to try to diffuse the situation.

"If you will allow me to speak, Ma'am" she began, "I answered the doorbell and saw Mr Heald standing there. I knew you were expecting the two doctors and could not understand why he was here. I did tell him it was inconvenient for him to see you today but he would not go away and practically forced his way in. As I turned to come to tell you about it, the doorbell rang again and it was the two doctors. I did not know what to do ma'am"

"Thank you, Hannah" Eliza sighed and sat down in a chair, her temper controlled. She looked at Mr Heald and all the trust she had ever placed in that man seemed to evaporate.

Sir Rickman Godlee spoke, sensing the tension and seeking the right words with which to diffuse the situation.

"My dear Mrs Macloghlin. Under the circumstances I think it is perhaps fortuitous that Mr Heald is here. While we were waiting for you he told us of the changes to your Will. As representative of the Royal College of Surgeons, who stand to benefit from your great generosity, we hope that any changes are not detrimental to us."

Eliza was in turmoil.

Surely the doctor would consider her health of greater importance than the terms of her Will. Surely the matter of her Will was a confidential issue between her and her solicitor.

Surely these men were totally wrong to be discussing these issues.

However, she smiled in her usual way and assured him that nothing would alter her oath to God or her promise to her husband and to the Royal College of Surgeons. However she intended to get rid of Mr Heald at once and instructed Hannah to show him out of the front door immediately.

Hannah stepped towards the door but Frederick Heald reached it first. He flung it open and turning to the assembled group, he wished them

Goodbye. Hannah left the room to see Mr Heald out of the house and Eliza settled down to consult with the doctors.

"I need you to know that my condition is desperate," she said. "I am so ill that some days I cannot leave my bed. The worst days are the ones when I take your prescribed medicines, Dr Price. On the days when I do not take them, such as today, I do still feel tired and irritable but I do not feel at the point of death. I know that I require some medication, but not that which you are prescribing. The Digitalis is poison to me."

Dr Price clenched his fists and pressed them into his knees. How dare this woman jeopardise his reputation by making such an accusation. She was insane. Anyone could see that. The stories her sister told proved it beyond all doubt. He did not know what to say.

Rickman Godlee was equally disturbed by her accusations and knew he needed to support his colleague. He also needed to reassure Eliza that he was on her side.

"I am sure you have nothing to fear from Dr Price, my dear. He is treating you well and appropriately. However, if it will put your mind at ease I will arrange for you to be attended by another colleague of mine. It may be necessary for you to spend a few days in hospital while we make some investigations. How would that suit you?"

Eliza was somewhat reassured by this. Perhaps if someone else were to treat her, the effects of this dreadful medicine would disappear.

"Thank you, thank you" she almost screamed "I knew I could depend upon you to be my Saviour"

"Well I must leave now as I have a very important engagement but I will set the wheels in motion for your admission to hospital"

Eliza thanked them both for coming and Hannah was summoned to see them out.

As they left, Margaret followed them and when she was sure that Eliza could neither see nor hear them she spoke quietly to the two men.

"I feel dreadful about this whole matter. My sister has been very kind and generous to me. She furnished a house for me and my children when my husband was in the asylum in Singapore. She has helped feed and clothe us all that time and I feel I owe her a debt of gratitude. I do not believe she owes me a penny and yet in her Will she has bequeathed to me most of her treasured possessions. I have no reason to complain at all and yet my father and brothers tell me all the time that what she is doing is wrong and must be opposed. I do not know what I should think or do."

"Are you talking about the alterations to her Will?" asked Dr Price.

"Well yes but also the fact that she has left so much to the Royal College of Surgeons and so little to the family. Do you think she really is mad?"

Dr Rickman Godlee realised now for the first time exactly what was happening. The family was opposed to her bequest to the College and was trying their best to prove that she was of unsound mind.

"Are you sure" he asked, in as kindly a manner as he could, "that there is not a hint of jealousy on your part? Could it not be that you envy your sister's wealth and way of life and would like it for yourself? You seem to be settling into this flat very nicely."

Margaret was mortified at such a suggestion but as she opened her mouth to reply Dr Price intervened.

"Not a bit of it, Margaret has only Eliza's best interests at heart. Do not worry about a thing. We will soon have your sister fit and well again and she will probably outlive you all"

This said, Margaret saw them from the house and went to her room.

Looking out of the window, Eliza saw the two men emerge from the front door of the Mansions and stand deep in conversation for several minutes. She wondered what they could be saying.

CHAPTER 9

Eliza had a strange feeling of apprehension when she awoke on the morning of June 2nd. She had felt so on previous occasions and knew that before the day was over she would have reason to understand why she felt thus. She believed above all else that the stars held her future and today the stars were telling her that those closest to her were not as close as she had believed.

Tomorrow it would be Alex's birthday and she was planning some surprises for him. She would never allow herself to lavish upon him the kinds of gifts she would upon his sister. She loved her nephew dearly but he was a boy. Men could look after themselves. She had found to her cost that men did not always appreciate women giving them gifts and that such actions were often misinterpreted. However, for her sister's sake and to give herself pleasure she had wrapped his presents carefully and written his birthday card. They were hidden away until tomorrow.

Margaret came into her room and opened the curtains. Although it was June, the day was dull and rain was in the air. There did not seem much to get out of bed for on days such as this. Eliza lay back on her pillows, the feelings of apprehension still causing her distress.

"Now then, sister dear" Margaret soothed," you stay there and I will bring you some tea and your medicine"

Eliza did not reply. She felt too weak and despondent for arguments. When Margaret returned with the tray, Eliza managed to sit up as the medicine glass was held out to her. Such bitter medicine it was. Surely her darling doctor Mac would never have allowed her to be forced to drink this disgusting mixture.

She took the dosage prescribed and then lay back again for a few minutes. The room seemed to be moving. She seemed to be floating above the bed. She closed her eyes and tried to compose herself. When she opened them, she was overcome by nausea. She must control this at all costs. Her body seemed to be floating upwards. Death that is what it was. She was moving towards Heaven and she would soon be with Mac. Then she saw Margaret standing by the bed and knew for certain that she had not died. She was only too alive.

"I think I will stay in bed today" she said weakly.

"As you wish" muttered Margaret. Tucking the blankets carefully around her sister, she left the room.

Eliza drank the tea her sister had brought and then lay down to rest. She awoke with a start as the bedroom door opened. Hannah came in and stood beside the bed.

"How are you feeling ma'am?" she inquired.

"Oh dear I seem to have been asleep. What time is it please?"

Hannah glanced at the clock, "Four thirty ma'am" she replied.

Four thirty! That special time of day when Mac had first made love to her and transported her into the heights of ecstasy. Her lips were moving in silent speech as she talked to Mac in her own mind. Hannah spoke but Eliza did not hear. She was far away in another time long past, wrapped in her lover's arms and giving herself to him as she would never give herself again."

Hannah was concerned that Eliza was in some sort of trance. She ran from the room and summoned Margaret.

"Mrs Street, the mistress is acting in a very strange manner, she does not seem to see or hear me, please come quickly"

Margaret hurried into the bedroom. Eliza did not move. The two women spoke to her but she did not hear. Margaret ran to fetch some more medicine and Eliza was persuaded to drink it. She closed her eyes and fell into another deep sleep.

Margaret decided that the doctors had been right. She was no longer able to care for Eliza herself. She telephoned Dr Price and asked him to come as soon as possible.

A nervous person at the best of times, Margaret was particularly restless for the rest of the afternoon. She could not sit down for long without looking out of the window to see whether the doctor was on his way. She walked about the room, rearranging ornaments, opening and closing drawers and endlessly checking on her sister. Eliza, however, was aware of none of this. She slept soundly as the afternoon turned into evening and as the long day darkened.

When the doorbell rang Margaret almost jumped out of her skin. As is often the case, however eagerly you have anticipated an event, it seems to take you by surprise when it actually happens.

Eliza woke at the sound of the doorbell and heard Dr Price's voice. Why was he here? Had Margaret summoned him while she slept? Then she heard another voice, not that of Dr Price, not the voice of anyone she knew. What was happening? She was gripped by panic. All day, or what part of it she had been aware of, she had had this dreadful foreboding. She tried to get out of bed but was too weak. She rang the bell by her bedside and Hannah answered it almost immediately.

"Has Dr Price arrived?"
"Yes ma'am and another doctor as well."
"Another doctor? Is it Sir Rickman Godlee?"

166

"No, ma'am, I think it is Dr Saunders. He has a surgery nearby. There are two nurses with them as well."

"Two nurses! Oh no, please Hannah, there is something dreadful happening to me. I do not trust any of them. My sister swore to me on the heads of her two children that she would never let these people into my flat again and she has done so."

Now Hannah was staring at Eliza in disbelief. Although her lips were moving, the sounds which came out of them made no sense. Then she heard Eliza say

"Please, go and fetch a Police Constable. Explain to him that these people have come to kill me. I know they will, please hurry, Go now!"

Hannah was almost moved to tears by Eliza's plight and determined to do whatever she could to help. She ran out of the front door and down the street until she saw a young police officer standing outside the Fire Station.

"Please will you come at once? My mistress fears she is about to be murdered"

"I am sorry Miss, but my duties are here at the Fire station. They do not include such matters. You need to go to the Police Station for that."

"Please come with me, I am sure the mistress will be reassured when she sees you"

She led the way hurriedly back to Eliza's flat and as they entered, Margaret and the two doctors were standing waiting for her.

"And what have we here?" exclaimed Dr Price.

Hannah was distraught. How could she explain why she had brought this police officer with her?

The young man himself rescued her from her dilemma.

"This young woman seems to think that a murder is about to be committed" he said with a laugh, "I could not ignore her pleas for help"

Dr Price stepped forward.

"Officer," he said calmly, "we are doctors and have come to remove the lady of this house to a nursing home where she will be cared for and returned to full health. We have brought two nurses with us to ensure she is treated well. Do we look like murderers? You can rest assured that we mean her no harm."

The policeman was convinced by their story and promised to do all he could to help.

Hannah however was still not convinced and far from happy. She had made a promise to Eliza and wanted her mistress to know that she had fulfilled that promise.

She pleaded with the doctor to allow Eliza to see that she had done as she asked and at length, after much deliberation, the two doctors agreed that Eliza should take the young man to meet her mistress.

As they entered, Eliza struggled to sit up but was unable to do so. She held out her hand to the young man.

"Thank you for coming so quickly" she whispered, "they are trying to kill me"

"I am sure they mean you no harm" he spoke in a kind and comforting manner.

"Oh yes they do. They all want my money and they get none of it until I am dead. I keep hoping to die so they will leave me alone but I don't die"

The doctors had crowded into the room behind Hannah and the policeman and now they moved towards the bed.

"My dear Mrs Macloghlin" said Dr Saunders," you agreed with Sir Rickman Godlee's suggestion that you go into hospital for some investigations into your condition. I am a friend of his and we have all the necessary papers for you to sign before we take you."

Eliza was horrified. She did not believe for one minute that this man was a friend of dear Sir Rickman. He was an impostor and only intent upon doing her harm.

"I need proper treatment, not papers to sign. If doctors had not been trying to poison me for the last year, I would not be in this bed now."

The doctors and Margaret spoke quietly together for a few minutes and Eliza thought that she need not be there at all for all the attention they were paying her. Had she become invisible and could nothing she said be heard by anyone else? She wanted to scream, to escape from that room, from that house, to run to her beloved Mac and lie safely in his arms.

She tried once more.

"Please will you leave me alone," she cried, "I feel quite sick and need to rest." She hoped that they would respect her privacy sufficiently to do as she asked. However, she was soon to realise that from that moment on, she would never enjoy the luxury of privacy again."

The young policeman was standing in the doorway looking completely confused by the situation into which he had been dragged. Eliza called out pitifully to him to stay and protect her. She felt alone, deserted and totally at the mercy of six determined people.

The doctors persuaded the policeman to stand outside the door of the flat while they attended their patient.

Eliza heard someone say 'bring some towels' and then her sister and the two nurses bound her in towels from head to foot, her arms held behind her back. They rolled her in a blanket and carried her from her bed, out of the flat and into a waiting taxicab. Once outside the door, she called out loudly "Murder! Murder!" for as far as she was concerned that is precisely what was taking place. However, the young policeman had been carefully briefed by the doctors and all he did was call out encouraging words as they carried her past him. "You will be all right, you will be all right"

Once inside the taxicab, one of the nurses forced Eliza's head back and covered her mouth with her hand.

As the taxi moved away, she managed to free her mouth and told Dr Price to loosen her.
"There is no need for violence, just tell me where you are taking me"

"To a nursing home" he answered and for a moment Eliza believed him. Then he continued, "You should not have said I was poisoning you". And then Eliza knew that his words had been lies and that they were indeed taking her to a Lunatic Asylum.

The taxi cab rumbled on for several miles, the longest miles Eliza had ever known. Her freedom removed, held in bonds and guarded by the two nurses, she wished for death more than ever. She resolved that wherever they took her, she would behave impeccably; giving no one any reason to suspect that she was insane. She would make them sorry for what they were trying to do to her. Finally the cab stopped. She heard the sound of feet running across the gravel and then the doors were opened. The lights of a building could be seen but she could not make out where they had brought her. The two nurses handled her roughly and she was dragged from the cab and carried bodily into the building. She felt cold, her feet were bare and she was wearing only a thin robe over her nightgown.

Finally she was taken into what appeared to be a doctor's consulting room. She looked desperately around her and realised that she was alone. Her captors had fled. She thought for a moment that she might be able to escape but knew that even if she were to leave this place she could no longer escape from those wishing to harm her. She tried to take in her surroundings, the bottles of medicine which stood on shelves and the many books which lined the walls all reminded her of Mac but as the door opened and the occupant of the room appeared, the man who now stood before her bore no resemblance whatsoever to her beloved doctor.

"Good evening, Mrs Macloghlin," The leering smile made her feel sick. What kind of place was this, she wondered.

"Good evening Doctor, would you please tell me where I am and why I have been brought here?" Eliza remembered her promise to herself, to be rational and polite at all times.

"Certainly, this is Hendon Court, a private nursing home for people like you I am the Director of the home and my name is Dr. De Caux."

The doctor sat at his desk and took out a pad on which to write notes. The room was cold and although Eliza shivered she was offered nothing to keep her warm. He pulled his chair close to Eliza and sat facing her. Eliza tried to pull her gown around her but it did not seem to reach. Her bare feet shook with cold. "Are you feeling cold, my dear?"

"Yes I am, I was not allowed time to put my clothes on before being brought here. The people who brought me had no right to do so." She thought he would realise from this that she had been forcibly removed from her home and would have some sympathy, but this was a vain hope. He smiled. He had heard this so many times before.

Dr De Caux asked Eliza about herself, her family and her home. He seemed interested in everything she said but never did he indicate that she should never have been brought here. The whole of that first interview with the doctor was to remain vividly in her memory for the rest of her life. She fought a losing battle throughout the conversation to make him see her as a sane person who was being wronged. He saw her as yet another wealthy inmate whose family wanted her out of the way. This one was a particularly beautiful specimen and possibly he might get to know her very well indeed. His unsavoury thoughts were not apparent to Eliza who was striving to earn his respect. She was horrified when he leaned forward and put his hand on her knee, gazing into her face all the time and moving his hand higher and higher up her thigh. She flung his hand away and got up from her chair.

"How dare you take such liberties with me"

"Liberties?" I cannot imagine what you mean. It is obvious that you are suffering from delusional disorder and we must begin treatment right away. Nurse!!"

Immediately, the door opened and two unpleasant looking women appeared.

"Take her away, this woman is extremely dangerous. Give her the usual medication and lock her away"

The women took hold of Eliza by her arms and led her, unprotesting, down the corridor and into a grimy bathroom. There she was ordered to remove all her clothing. The moment's hesitation was sufficient excuse for the women to take matters into their own hands and Eliza was nauseated as she felt the hands of these two rough women tearing at her clothes and touching her naked body. One of them noticed the scar on her abdomen, the result of her Hysterectomy.

" What was that for?" she was asked

"It was an operation to prevent me having children" she replied calmly

"You'll be glad you had that then, once you're in here"

"Why on earth should that matter to anyone in here?" Eliza questioned naively.

The two women laughed uproariously at her innocence.

"Wait till you've met the doctor a few more times, then you'll understand. Time for your medicine my dear"

Eliza had suffered for so long from the effects of medication that she was wary of taking anything they offered her. The tablet they thrust into her hand was familiar but Eliza could not place what it was.
"What exactly is this?"
The two women mimicked her refined tones.

"Well actually it is a tablet" they both laughed loud and long at this

"Yes I can see that but what is it for, you see I have a weak heart"

"Really? Well this won't harm you, it is a.. (The woman gave this some thought).. laxative, yes, that is what it is, a laxative"

Eliza did not like the idea of being given aperients but she took it with a drink of water, offered to her in a dirty enamel cup.

Then she was told to leave the bathroom and follow them down the corridor.

"But I have no clothes on, people might see me"

"So they might, but they won't care"

This must have been the most distressing time of her life up to that moment. She followed them in a distraught state and they pushed her into a room and locked the door.

Once inside, Eliza was sickened by the unbearable stench of human excrement and urine. She huddled in a corner and began to weep quietly. The silent sobs grew louder and soon she was weeping noisily and uncontrollably, her whole body shaking. Gradually the sobs subsided and she fell asleep.

When she awoke, she hoped it had all been a horrible dream but as she became fully awake she began to take in her surroundings. There was a small barred window high up near the ceiling and through this filtered the bright June sunlight. The light cast shadows around this prison room and onto its wretched occupant. Eliza's body gleamed white against the filth that surrounded her and she wondered what it reminded her of. She smiled to herself as the thought came to her. The white marble floor in the Royal College of Surgeons. She began to laugh and the nurse opening the door took it to be the inane laughter of a mad woman. This nurse appeared kind enough and seemed to show some concern for Eliza's well being. She was not the same nurse she had seen the previous day. She brought her food and water to wash and allowed her to go to the lavatory. Eliza was then locked away to contemplate the events, which had led to this.

As the day wore on, Eliza wondered how many other people were in this place. How many of them were mad and how many the victims of the greed of their families? Food and drink was brought at regular intervals throughout the day and then, towards evening, as far as Eliza could make out by the passage of the sun across the small patch of sky visible through the bars, she was ordered out of the room and into the bathroom once more. There she was forced into a bath, scrubbed and given first of all a grubby shift to wear and then another of the tablets she had so reluctantly taken the previous night. Since it did not appear to have had any laxative effect, Eliza presumed that it must be some harmless substance and took it willingly.

Then she was led into a cleaner, brighter room where she had a mattress to lie on and access to a bathroom nearby. That night she slept soundly and only awoke when the nurse brought her some breakfast.

Although Eliza valued the privacy afforded her by this room, she wished she could have someone to speak to. However, she saw nobody, spoke to no one apart from the nurses who brought her meals.

Eliza asked to see the doctor again, stressing that she did not want to see him alone but in the company of one of the nurses.

She was led into Dr De Caux's office. He smiled as she entered.
"Thank you nurse, you may leave us now" he said cheerily.

"No she cannot," cried out Eliza, hysterically, "I said I did not want to see him by myself"

"I said, thank you, nurse" repeated the doctor.

The nurse left the room and Eliza turned to follow her but as she did so the doctor took hold of Eliza from behind and held her in a fierce grip. He turned her round and pressed his lips firmly on hers, holding her arms tightly behind her back with one hand. His other hand explored her body roughly and with no grace. Eliza released her mouth and bit him hard on his chin.

As he squealed in pain, the nurse entered the room.

"Take this woman away" he screamed. "Put her in the padded cell.

Eliza had heard of such places but never expected to see the inside of one. Now she was taken to the most dreadful place she had ever seen. Thrust inside, her clothes removed from her again and locked in; she wished she could die. Panic seized hold of her and she began to scream loudly. No one answered her screams and so she began to shout for the doctor. As she became more and more afraid, she found it difficult to control her bodily functions and soon she realised that the smell she abhorred was coming from her. She wanted to clean herself, but with what? She tore at the padding on the walls to try to get something to wipe herself with, but only succeeded in breaking her fingernails. That this beautiful woman, used as she was to wearing the most expensive clothes money could buy, to having her hair dressed by the finest hairdressers and her nails manicured each week, should be reduced to this. She screamed out to try to make people understand what she was suffering but no one came; no one cared why she was making such a noise. For two nights and two days Eliza was locked in that room and then finally, worn out with screaming and shouting she gave in to her fate. Once sufficient time had elapsed since Eliza had stopped screaming, the door opened and the two nurses, who Eliza had learned were called Nurse Ethel Hicks and Nurse Lizzie Davies, came in to Eliza. Nurse Hicks carried two papers in her hand which she offered to Eliza and asked her if she could read them.

"Indeed yes," she told her and Eliza read both papers through out loud. They were official orders, which she must sign before midnight if she wished to see a magistrate. She certainly did wish to see the magistrate. Here she had found herself, an invalid with a tired heart, in Hendon Grove where she had no place at all. She was being ill-treated and put in an almost airless padded room. Now she was being given a chance of salvation, a hearing by a magistrate. "Of course I will sign them" she said quickly," would you be so kind as to give me a pen and some ink"

The nurses stood silently watching her, listening as the footsteps they recognised approached. The door opened and there stood Doctor de

Caux. This time Eliza could hardly believe her eyes. On one shoulder sat a tiny grey monkey, on the other a parrot. She tried to ignore these and asked him for the necessary items so she could sign the papers. However, the doctor refused her request and held out his hand for the papers back. Eliza refused to return the papers unsigned and so with a shrug he turned and left the padded room followed by the two nurses. Left alone with the two papers, Eliza's thoughts turned to the desperate measures she would need to sign these papers. It was impossible even to make a thumbprint signature. She thought she might double the paper where her name ought to be and bite so as to leave an impression of her front teeth. However, she doubted whether anyone would understand her intentions. She resigned herself to the fact that she was in the hands of a man who was obviously deranged and who would not let her see a magistrate at any price. She went over to the door of the padded room, slipped a corner only of the folded papers underneath the door and called out pleadingly, "Please bring me a pen and ink, these papers are no use to me unless you will bring me a pen and ink" The papers were immediately snatched away out of her fingers.

At about ten o'clock the following morning, Eliza was taken from the padded room and given an overall to wear. She was allowed no undergarments. She was taken not to her own room but to that of an old deranged woman called Mrs. Walker. The old lady talked loudly and incomprehensibly all day long. She was never still but walked around all day. Eliza was made to lie on a couch in the old lady's room until six o'clock at night. Then she was led back to the padded room and her clothes removed. This was repeated for the next three days. Eliza imagined that they were hoping that she would become violent once more and thus give them more reason to ill treat her. However she did not give them this satisfaction. She screamed no more, and tore no more. The episode with the papers had broken her spirit and she decided to await her fate. Eventually, she was sure, sense would prevail, they would realise that she was not mad and had no reason to be there and she would be released and return home. Of that there was no doubt.

On the tenth of June she was taken once more to Mrs. Walker's room. She prepared herself for another day of the old woman's ramblings and incessant walking about, touching Eliza's hair and tugging at her clothing. Eliza was not allowed to speak to the lady nor to call out and she felt that even if she were not mad when she came into this place she very soon would be. At first, Mrs. Walker behaved in her usual manner, and then she sat on the floor by Eliza's bed and fell asleep. Eliza was grateful for this until it became apparent that the old woman was not asleep but dead. She called out for someone to come but no one came. After she had tried two or three times to attract someone's attention, a voice called through the door to her telling her to be quiet or she would be sent back to the padded room.

Eliza spent the whole of that day with the body of the old woman at the side of her bed. When in the evening they came to take her back to her cell, Eliza was silently weeping. That night they allowed her to sleep once more in her own room, room number 8. Each day she begged to be allowed paper and pen so that she could write to her friends, although she had by now realised that she could trust no one with her friendship.

Days passed in the same way. Each night she was given yet another of the so-called aperient tablets but Eliza doubted that this was what they were. The next day she received a visit from her sister Margaret. Her first thought was that Margaret had realised that a mistake had been made and that this was a Lunatic Asylum and not a Nursing Home. As soon as Eliza saw her however, she realised that she was wrong. Margaret had not come to take her home.

"Sister, dear" Margaret began, but she was not allowed to continue.

"Sister Dear? How dear can I be to you who have sent me to this place?"

Margaret averted her eyes, too ashamed to look at the wretched creature who she could hardly recognise as her beautiful sister.

"Why did you let them do this to me, I trusted you, I looked after you, brought you into my home and lavished gifts upon you." Eliza was bitter and this bitterness frightened Margaret.

"You were ill, Eliza, you did strange things and we could not look after you anymore."

"Strange things, you mean like giving you my clothes and my treasures, like buying you a house and furnishing it for you. Yes those are very strange things indeed for a sister to do."

Margaret went on "But you kept upsetting us."

"I kept upsetting you? How did I do that?"

"You kept on saying you were going to die, and... you did not die"

Eliza was dumbfounded. How could they have been upset because she did not die?
Gradually the reality of the situation dawned upon her. It was the Will. Once she was dead they could begin to contest it, to try to get more for themselves and less for the Royal College of Surgeons. They could do nothing while she was still alive. Margaret had been sent to live with her so that she could have some chance of persuading Eliza to change her Will, but this had not worked. Now they had to prove that she was insane and so get the matter resolved that way.

"I want you to go away and never come back" Eliza had never felt so betrayed in her life.
As Margaret turned to go, Eliza called her back
"I would like you to send me detailed accounts of all the money which you have spent of mine while you have been living in my house."

After her sister had gone, Eliza sat down and re-lived all the years that had passed since she had first met her beloved Mac. In all that time her family had wanted her only for what she could offer them. They had taken her gifts and her money but they had given nothing in return. Her tyrannical father, her weak spineless mother, her brothers who lived only for themselves had never been there when she had needed them. During the long years which led up to Mac's death she had had no support or comfort from them and once alone they saw her only as a means of becoming rich one day. She had foiled this by bequeathing the bulk of her estate to the Royal College of Surgeons and for this they could not and would not forgive her.

The nurse brought in her evening tablet but Eliza refused to take it. Whatever it was, she was sure it was blurring her senses, making it more difficult for her to think rationally and think rationally she must if she was to survive.

Once Eliza refused to take any more of the tablets, the medication was offered in the form of a glass of milk turned blue by the addition of some substance. When she refused to drink it, the nurse called for help and between them they forced the evil liquid down Eliza's throat. She fell into a drugged sleep. On awakening, she was given a further dose and once this had worn off she found herself unable to stand properly or see straight. She vowed she would take no more of the filthy stuff. She learned how to deal with this liquid. She would ask permission to go to wash her hands. Once her hands were well soaped she would fill her hands with water and then, appearing to wash her face she would drink as much of the soapy water as she could. This acted as an emetic and she was soon vomiting the poison out of her system. She suspected that this secret, but immediate antidote to the poison worked until it was discovered.

On the 16th of June she realised that life in Hendon Grove could not be tolerated. She knew she was not the usual type of patient there but that there was no way out for her, alive. To remain in Hendon Grove meant madness. Until that afternoon suicide had never entered her mind but now she saw that it was her only way out.

Alone in her room she looked down at the ivory skin on her arms, with the delicate blue veins running along. Lifting up her arm she bit as hard as she could, through the vein. As the blood began to flow she took a safety pin from her skirt and pushed it into the wound. The pain was nothing compared to the knowledge that soon it would all be over. She began to thread the pin along the vein in the manner of threading a cord through a garment. She could not be sure how far she could go but hoped in time the pin would reach her poor heart and put an end to her misery.

The door opened and the nurses entered. Seeing Eliza covered in blood she called for the doctor and together they began to bind her wound. The doctor noticed the shape of the safety pin under her skin and taking a scalpel from his bag he removed it painfully. Eliza's screams were music to their ears. She had done what they hoped she would do and proved to them that she was indeed insane. However her actions had in fact saved her in some way for the tablets were now withdrawn.

It was some time later that Eliza met the Matron of Hendon Court, a kind woman who recognised that many of her patients were, like Eliza, there under false pretenses. She tried to talk to the doctor about her fears and misgivings but he persuaded her that she was there to do a job and not question his authority. Matron and Eliza were two intelligent women and as such were able to talk freely to each other. She told Eliza that the tablets had been Veronal, a sedative used to control violent patients. Given over a prolonged period they caused the inmates to accept their fates and settle down. This, Eliza suspected, was what their families wanted.

Eliza admitted that she regretted this suicide attempt. She realised that she was under observation at all times. Anything she did was noted and used as testimony to her insanity. She decided there and then that observe her as they might they would not see any change in her.

On the 24th of June she received a visit. It was Mr. Frederic Heald. At first she thought he had come to take her home, but he had merely come to seal her fate still further, by issuing an "In Lunacy Summons".

Eliza was frantic when this was issued. However much she tried she was unable to control her temper. This in turn was construed as indisputable evidence of her insanity. The sheer frustration created in her by the situation was more than she could tolerate. She collapsed, trembling on the floor and was carried away, back to serve her sentence.

When she awoke, calmer now, the reality of her fate became clear. Now she was officially insane. The victim they said, of Chronic Mania, she would not be allowed to conduct her own affairs; they could sell her property and share the spoils among them. She begged to see Matron.

Matron reassured her that she need not worry about such things happening she still had the protection of the law and it would be a long, long time before there was any danger of her property being sold. Matron was in no doubt that with careful nursing, Eliza would quite soon be able to prove herself capable of leaving the asylum and would be entrusted once more with the conduct of her affairs.

Eliza felt sure that if someone would fix a date for her discharge, however far away this might be, then she would manage to survive being there; but to remain there indefinitely was more than she could comprehend and induced such sadness that she felt her heart would break.

Eliza spent three more weeks trying to come to terms with what had happened to her. She slept as much as she could because this shortened the days; the sedatives they gave her helped her to sleep the rest of the time. There seemed no way out of the situation. Everyone was against her and it became clear to her when she lay on her narrow bed and tried to reconstruct the events which had led up to that dreadful night of June 2nd, that there were too many people intent upon keeping her out of the way.

She had proved herself responsible enough to be allowed a few privileges. One of these was that she was allowed to use a typewriter. She decided that she would write to the few people on Earth who might be sympathetic, she would give them the facts of the case and trust that they would do all they could to help her. She knew that her letters would be scrutinized before she was allowed to send them but she was confident that they would contain only the truth and who could argue against that.

The first letter she wrote was to her solicitor; Not to Frederic Heald whom she suspected of being a party to the treachery but to his brother John in Wigan on whose advice she had become involved with Frederic.

'Dear Mr. Heald' she wrote

'It is nearly beyond belief that you are my Solicitor, lately so interested in telling me to 'take care of your nice self'; interested in telling me to 'spend all your money on yourself - interest and capital' that 'The Royal College of Surgeons don't care two snaps for you, nor anyone else' interested in telling me to 'leave your money to them that have done you a good turn'

Eliza paused in her writing to reflect on who these people might be who had done her this good turn. She supposed he thought he himself might be in for a share of the money. She continued

"That I can be ordered away to a Lunatic Asylum by my sister Mrs. Margaret Street, a feeble creature as you know, who was a guest in my house at the time, persuaded by doctors Into believing anything they told her. And you leave me to my fate absolutely. Yes it is nearly beyond belief after the grateful letters I have written you and my many gifts to you over and above your charges ever since October 19th 1909."

She outlined in the letter the events leading up to the night of June 2nd leaving out nothing of the way she felt his brother had treated her.

"I have received an account from my sister Mrs. Street of the money she spent of mine while she was a guest in my flat, and I was not there, but here, and your brother's name appears in the account, 'Mr. Heald - £2' What's that for, I wonder? The next time I saw your brother - the last time I saw him was on June 24th when he came to this Hendon Grove and served me with an 'In Lunacy Summons' I told him the thing was a crime against truth which it certainly was. I told him to send for you at once, which he agreed to do, and to bring my father and mother and we would go into this 'In Lunacy Summons'

As she reached this point in the letter, she was conscious of someone reading over her shoulder. She turned to see Matron standing there.
"I'm afraid you won't be allowed to send that letter, Mrs. MacLoghlin" she said.
"Why on earth not? I don't mind it being read before it goes and you will see that there is nothing wrong with it"
"The doctor will decide whether there is anything wrong in it, but you may only write to your blood relations."
Eliza was stunned. Her blood relations - those ignorant helpless people who had put her there in the first place.

"Oh well I will still write the letters and then perhaps one day when I am free I can give them to the people personally"

She continued with the letter
"You have treated me badly, cruelly indeed not to come at once to see me as soon as you knew what doctors and my sister Mrs. Street had done with me, to rescue me in case I was not a lunatic!
Only approved letters are allowed out of this Lunatic Asylum: I might not write to my Solicitor - no, nor to anyone at all except my strange blood relations.

Eliza seethed inwardly but controlled her urge to scream at him. Screaming was an indication of madness, she had found.

She continued to put the letter in its envelope, addressed it to John Heald and put it safely in her bag. Then she returned to her room.

The next day, she waited with growing impatience for the arrival of dear, kindly Dr. Mott.

She decided to write some more letters and he could post them all for her. She saw Dr. De Caux and Matron walking out in the gardens and thought this would be a good time to write.

Why had she not thought of it before, the one man who would not want her to be regarded as insane, Sir Rickman Godlee, President of the Royal College of Surgeons?

"Dear Sir Rickman J. Godlee"

Eliza sat, pen poised in her hand, planning what she should say to the great and good man. So much had happened to her in the past few years. Events had overtaken her and she realised now that she had been too trusting, too gullible. She had believed that her sister and even her father and brothers had really wanted what was best for her. Now she knew for certain that they were only interested in what they could get out of her. The moment when she came to this conclusion was one which brought fear into her heart. She was totally at the mercy of those who had put her in this dreadful place. She wondered whether she would ever been in control of her own life again.

She finished the letter in which she outlined all her suspicions and fears and pleaded that he might use his influence to order that she be returned to the real world once more. Again, this letter, and others which she wrote, were not approved by the authorities and she stored them away, hoping that one day her father might visit her, feel some sort of contrition for her plight and post the letters for her.

This was not to be, for even when he did finally visit her and agreed to take the letters he did not post them. It was to be several years before she recovered them.

185

In September, three months after she had arrived at Hendon Grove, she was summoned to the doctor's office.

"We have decided that we can do no more for you here, Mrs. Macloghlin. I am sorry you refuse to cooperate with us here, I'm sure we could have learned to work together but it was not to be."

The doctor, (she could hardly bring herself to call him a doctor, implying as this did that he was of the same breed as her own, dear dead Mac) looked at the pathetic woman and almost felt sorry for her. There were so many here like her, victims of greed and weakened by sobbing and sleepless nights. He felt some remorse on occasions for the way he was forced to treat them but he had his own needs to satisfy. He had acquired for himself a lavish lifestyle, built on the proceeds of this place. He did not intend to sacrifice that for the sake of a few scruples. He was only too aware that should he turn away these people they would only go somewhere else.

In the case of Eliza he felt that she was too well connected for him to keep her here any longer. He had read the letters she insisted on writing. She had written on the last occasion to Scotland Yard and he knew that should she succeed in getting these letters out, investigations might begin and he might find himself having to answer some very awkward questions. He had decided to allow her to go ahead with her pleas for release. He felt that in her present state she would only manage to incriminate herself even further. The result would, he hoped, be to send her elsewhere.

The next months were filled for Eliza with interviews, examinations, more and more discussions and frustration at every one. She who had led a more independent life than most women of her day was now incarcerated and deemed incapable of making the simplest decision for herself. Never in this whole time did she lose sight of the fact that she was sane and that her family, from a motive of greed, was managing the whole affair. This knowledge kept her from giving in to them.

However, it became apparent to her that if she was ever to have physical freedom again this would be at the cost of her freedom of movement and management of her affairs. She finally agreed to the settlement of her money in the hands of the Public Trustee. He would be responsible for investing the capital and for paying Eliza the income from this. She was to report regularly to her Trustee and in return she was to be allowed to return to her own home.

CHAPTER 10

On February 9th 1915, almost 2 years after that dreadful night which would live forever in her memory, Eliza returned to her flat.

Once home again, Eliza tried to pick up the pieces of her life. She engaged a maidservant to keep the flat clean and to cook her meals. This, along with every other expense incurred had to be approved by the Public Trustee. However, this was a small price to pay for being free from the torment of the asylum.

Her health had deteriorated during the time she had been away. She was weak and depressed and her hearing was severely impaired. She rarely left the house and few visitors called. News of her plight reached the members of society who once were proud to boast of their friendship with the infamous Mrs. MacLoghlin but they were now too embarrassed by Eliza's problems to associate with her.

The days were long, she read and slept and wrote letters to her friends and those whom she could trust. Whenever she spoke to her Trustee he would try to persuade her to give up her flat and move somewhere else, somewhere where she would not have to spend so much time alone with her thoughts. She held on for as long as she could to the idea that she would soon be her old self again but one thing stood in her way, she knew that her days as a free thinking, independent woman were over, she had been ill-used and would never feel able to trust anyone again.

One day Eliza received a visit from a young woman of about thirty years of age. She had heard of Eliza's plight from a mutual acquaintance and had decided to offer help. Her name was Christine and she ran a refuge for homeless refugees and widows and orphans of the war. Her own husband had been in Germany at the outbreak of war and had been interned there. Now she hoped to do what she could for people in similar situations over here.

The refuge was in a beautiful English country House near Osterley Park, called Holland House.

Eliza was pleased to receive a visit from a kind stranger and the two women became friends from the start. Christine came to see her on several occasions before suggesting to her that she visit Holland House for herself. She accepted the invitation and, after that, visited the House often and made many friends there. It was a house full of hope and kindness. There were few restrictions except those necessary for the smooth running and mutual comfort of the inhabitants.

The children there loved her and called her 'Aunty Mac' they liked her soft, gentle voice and the way she sat and told them stories or sang to them.

There were well-tended gardens around the house and it was there that she found peace and her mind began to recover from the ache which had been there for the last few years. Eventually, Christine offered Eliza a home in the house if she so wished. She would have her own flat within the house and would be able to assist in the running of the place. Her Trustee thought this an admirable solution to her problem. She needed time to consider this suggestion and spent many days deliberating the pros and cons.

One day as she was sitting in the garden she was surprised to find herself joined by a young soldier. He looked miserable and dejected. Eliza spoke to him

"I can see you are very unhappy, young man, is there anything I can do to help?"

The young man looked up in surprise. It was highly unusual for a woman of her breeding to start a conversation with a strange man.

"Is it quite so obvious?" he asked, trying to smile.

"I have spent too much time feeling unhappy myself not to recognise those same feelings in others". Eliza was pleased to be able to offer comfort, and wished someone had been able to do the same for her.

"I am in no worse condition than many others" he said "I am recovering from injuries received in action and I will soon be returning to the front. I just wish the whole wretched war would end and free us all from the misery it is causing"

"Why are you here in the gardens, do you live here?" she asked

The young man looked disturbed

.

"No I do not live here, I realise that I am trespassing but this is such a peaceful place and no one has ever taken any notice of me before"

"What about your family?" she asked.

"I have no family. My parents both died many years ago. I have been in hospital in England and I suppose I could stay there until I return to the front. That should be quite soon"

"Come with me" Eliza took command.

Taking his arm, she walked with him to the front door of Holland House.

"Leave this to me," she said, "and do not look surprised by anything I say"

Leading him into the hallway of the house she bade him take a seat. He was still rather confused by what was happening and sat, stunned, on a carved oak seat.

Eliza was away for a few minutes and then returned and sat down beside him.

"I have just realised that I do not even know your name, nor you mine" she giggled with her girlish giggle she had not known for years.

"Percy" he said sheepishly, "Percy Smith"

Eliza stared at him and the years rolled away. Percy! 'Edward Percy Plantagenet MacLoghlin, do you take this woman to be your lawful wedded wife?' the words still rang in her mind.

"Oh I do, I do" she said aloud and then realised with a start that this young man was staring at her in disbelief and wondering whether she was quite right in the head.

"Oh I do apologise" she said with a strange, embarrassed laugh. "You must think I am mad - and you would not be the first to think so, but I can assure you I am quite sane. No, Percy was my dear late husband's name and hearing it again brought back such memories that I was quite carried away"

They were joined by Christine. Eliza introduced Percy as the son of a friend of hers and requested that he might be given a room in the house until the time came for his return to the Front. There was no hesitation, here was kindness itself.

Eliza decided now that she would indeed be well advised to move into this house herself and be happy. She would move in immediately and then arrange for her flat to be sold and her belongings either stored or sold if she could not take them with her. She now felt happier than she had done in years; she became fitter and less tired and took delight in tending to the poor deserted people in Holland House.

She saw much of Percy Smith during those early days. He was many things to her, He was her son, the child she had never had, the brother she wished she could be close to her and, in her mind, he was the lover she had lost. Percy, for his part was grateful to Eliza and treated her with the love he would have saved for his mother. Percy was not to be there very long, however. He received papers telling him to return to the front. Eliza was sad to see him go, as were the children and others at Holland House. They had all loved him and wished him well.

For his part he went away knowing he had found love and friendship for the first time in a long time.

Now Eliza found yet more reason to feel unhappy once more. A letter arrived which she hardly dared to open. It was, as she suspected, from her ex-Solicitor, Mr. John Heald. He had heard that Eliza was now out of the hands of the Lunacy people and he was offering his services once more as her Solicitor. Rage boiled within her as she read and re-read the letter. How dare this man, whose brother had actually helped her sister and the doctor to send her to the Asylum, now offer the hand of friendship.

It was several weeks before Eliza could bring herself to reply and when she did so it was in the most courteous vein that she thanked him for his offer but felt obliged to refuse it at that time. Once her reply had been posted she relaxed and hoped she would hear no more of the matter. She knew that should she give the slightest hint of vindictiveness or paranoia she would stand little chance of remaining free for long. She decided that she would leave her fiat. At least if she were away from there she would not be haunted by the memories of that dreadful night. John Heald was not to be put off so easily. Letter after letter arrived from him at 40 Ashworth Mansions, most of which lay unanswered upon Eliza's desk. The replies she did write were identical in content. She did not feel able to accept his offer of help at this time.

Finally, she felt as though the tightly coiled spring which she had been holding in check for so long, unleashed itself. She put pen to paper during a period of rage and left John Heald in no doubt as to the reasons why she would not engage him. His brother, she informed him, had helped the doctor and Mrs. Street to commit her to a Lunatic Asylum. He was but a feeble criminal to have a hand in such frightfulness.

On receipt of the letter John Heald did what he considered the only thing to do in the circumstances, he forwarded the letter immediately to his brother.

Frederick Heald was not surprised to receive the letter; he had half expected it for some time and was prepared for what he must do next. Meanwhile, arrangements were well in hand for the disposal of Eliza's property either by auction or to safe storage until such time as she was able to have a home of her own in which to display it once more. There was much to be done, but even more to be done at Holland House. There were children crying for their fathers and mothers. Sick children who, because they were poor, were at the mercy of the doctors who would treat them free of charge.

One little four-year-old boy, whom Eliza called Mim, lay deathly white on his bed. His adenoids had been removed and he had almost bled to death. Eliza wondered whether the doctor who performed this dirty and inept operation had known that his father was a German who had been interned in England for the duration of the war. He was being sheltered by Christine, along with his sister and their grandmother. There was no feeling of animosity among these people whose countries were at war, just love for fellow human beings.

Meanwhile, the boy's mother was an actress playing at that time in Birmingham. She had had to leave her child in the care of Christine while she earned sufficient money to enable them both to live. Eliza pondered upon the feelings of that poor woman, playing to an audience, hiding her real heartache behind a facade of laughter. Her spirit in a room in Holland House gazing sadly down on this pale, still child, wishing she could kiss him and help him back to health.

Shortly after she had taken up residence at Holland House she received a letter from Mr. John Heald. It was a writ for Libel. Libel! She had told only the truth, she would have no case to answer of that she was sure.

193

However, according to the paper, which lay on the desk in front of her, the libel action was to be heard on April 6th 1916, in two months time. She now needed to find herself a Solicitor to help her fight this charge. She went to see her Trustee to ask his advice as to which Solicitor she should choose.

"That is something over which you have no control, Mrs. Macloghlin" the Trustee said.
"We must find one for you, one of whom we approve" Eliza realised once more that she no longer had control of her life. How often had she felt like this over the years? First her father, then her beloved Doctor had controlled her. For a brief spell she had felt the thrill of independence but that was short-lived.

The weeks passed and still she heard nothing from her Trustee as to which Solicitor had been selected. Surely she needed to speak with him, put her side of the story to him, give him chance to prepare the case, and it was already the end of March.
On April 3rd, less than two weeks before the case was to be heard, Eliza received a telegram from the chosen Solicitor. She was to see him in his office on that very day.

Eliza wasted no time. She took sufficient money in her purse to enable her to pay any fees required of her and took the train to the address on the telegram. As she travelled to the appointment, she began to have a dreadful feeling of apprehension. It was not beyond the realms of possibility that this new Solicitor was in league with the Lunacy people in wanting to see her back in the Asylum. She fought to put such ideas out of her head but by the time she reached the office she was in a state of turmoil. As she crossed the threshold of the office, suddenly without any warning, she collapsed, unconscious in a heap on the floor. It lasted for only a few seconds and she tried to compose herself in order to conduct the business for which she was there. She apologised profusely for having fainted and was aware of the look of despair and embarrassment on the face of the man she had come to see. No sooner had she seated herself in the chair and begun to explain the matter of the Libel action, than she fainted again.

As she recovered consciousness and looked around her she saw two men bending over her, one was the Solicitor, a stranger to her before this meeting, the other was no stranger. She could scarcely breathe as the reality of the situation became apparent. A doctor had evidently been called when she had fainted again. As she lay there, trying to focus her eyes upon the two faces above her, she could only be more and more certain that one of them was that of Dr. Price, the doctor who had been present on the night she had been dragged out of her flat.

Although Eliza was sure it was that man, he gave no indication that he knew Eliza and after a cursory examination of her, declared that she would be fit to continue with the interview. He sat quietly by while she and the Solicitor continued with the appointed business. However, Eliza's thoughts were racing. Why was this man here? What had he said? What lies had he told? Perhaps he was waiting until she left before he told the Solicitor that Eliza was of unsound mind and not to be believed. No attempt had been made to help her over what was obviously a traumatic situation. It was as if fainting was in some way as big a crime as committing libel and one for which she must pay dearly.

The solicitor asked her details regarding the letter she had written to Frederic Heald and her reasons for doing so. She outlined the events which had terminated in her writing a letter she had not intended to write. Although he seemed satisfied with her explanation, Eliza was disturbed by the presence of Dr Price in the room, listening to everything she said.

As she got up to leave, the doctor offered her a glass of water and a small tablet.

"Here take this and sit outside the office for a while before you attempt to make the journey home, it will help relax you"

He seemed too kind to be the same man who had been party to the dreadful events of June 12th. Perhaps she was mistaken, much had happened to confuse her mind since then. She thanked him and took the tablet with the water. Bidding 'Goodbye' to the two men she left the room and as had been suggested she sat on a seat on the landing outside the office. After a few minutes the two men left and hoped she would be alright.

That was at 5.30 in the afternoon.

The events of the next twenty-four hours were never absolutely clear to Eliza. It appeared that she had fallen into some sort of trance as she stood on the stairs in that office block. She told herself many times over that she ought to have left immediately after the two men had gone, and taken the first train home. She could not imagine why she did not do so. She must have thought she needed longer to recover from her distressing experiences that afternoon.

Whatever the reason, she stood there, unable to speak or move. Aware of trying to do so and being unable to. She thought of the words of her poem 'Paralysis', and knew that what she was feeling now must have been how her beloved doctor had felt. She dreamed, if dreaming is how thoughts while in a state of trance, are described. In her dream, voices were talking to her

"Percy is dead," they repeated. Percy? Percy Smith? Percy dead? "Percy is killed" they repeated with more urgency. As she lay there, conscious but still and rigid she wondered about Percy.

Aware of what was happening but unable to move or speak was the worst situation Eliza could imagine. But it was happening now. She heard the voice of Dr. Price in her ear. "Come, come Mrs. Macloghlin, you cannot stay here, it is ten o'clock at night, we must get you away from here"

There was money in her purse, almost nineteen pounds, they could call a cab, but they did not. She felt her clothes being taken off in a rough fashion, she could not bear to think of these hands touching her body, holding her the way they did. She was unable to resist in any way. She felt herself being manhandled down the stairs, felt the cold rush of air as she was carried out into the street and then smelled the foul smell of a dirty tarpaulin being wrapped around her as she was dumped unceremoniously in a ramshackle wooden hand cart, the type with two wheels and two legs. A canvas was flung over her and she was trundled at a run over the stones, over the rough and over the smooth. She could only think that she was being taken to Hell.

The trance lasted for twenty-four hours. Finally she came out of it quite naturally and as she did so became aware of her surroundings. She was in Fulham Road Workhouse. Why had they not used her money to take her to Charing Cross Hospital, which was only across the road from the office block? Why? Because Dr. Price had wanted her out of the way, had needed her out of the way to prevent the scandal of the libel case. He needed her to be certified and that is what had happened while she lay in her cataleptic trance.

The nightmare had begun again. Once more the assessments, the questions, the inhuman treatment. No clothes of her own, no visitors, only other pathetic creatures like herself for company.

She was given an appalling workhouse frock to wear and huge uncomfortable boots. Some of the women there were so mentally ill they could not even fasten their bootlaces and Eliza was pleased to be able to do it for them. There was a disgustingly filthy room full of basins where they were supposed to wash themselves. No one cared whether they did so or not and Eliza was nauseated by the stench of poverty and stale perspiration. She washed the frock she had been given to wear and did the same for the other women. She rinsed the pathetic rags clean of the harsh soap which remained in them. She showed them how to shake out the rags and freshen them. Then she washed and dried the basins and taps and the poor imbeciles watched her. Some of them copied what she did. She showed them how to comb out their dirty hair brushes matted with hair. In these small ways she felt she was giving them some dignity in their very undignified lives.

Tired and weary, she lay down on a horsehair sofa in the common room and one of the so-called lunatics came and put a chair against the sofa to prevent her from falling off. The woman began to cry. Eliza was so touched by this small act of kindness that she got up at once from the sofa and went to talk to her, sitting beside her on a chair. However, weak as she was, Eliza fell off the chair at the woman's feet. She could not help herself from fainting. When she eventually awoke she was naked and wrapped in blankets lying on a mattress on the floor of a filthy stinking padded vault. For the next ten days she remained there, starved nearly to the point of death and beaten until her body was covered with wounds and bruises. She had been so badly beaten about the head that her already impaired hearing had been irreparably damaged. This affliction was to haunt her for the rest of her days.

When she met Leonard Fulton of the Public Trustee's office she pleaded with him to help her. When he tried to explain that he could not, she flew into a rage, screaming abuse at him and ordering him out. Not deterred by this, his next action was to have Eliza transferred to a different Asylum. Eliza sat in her room and, in desperation, wrote to her father. She could not bear the thought of living once more under his roof but she knew it must be better than this. She pleaded with him to be her Receiver and Petitioner again, to take responsibility for her and take her home with him.
She promised she would be good and live according to his rules. She awaited his reply eagerly, confident that he would show compassion on his eldest daughter and receive her once more into the bosom of his family. Eliza was aghast as she read his eventual reply. All he said was "Is your Will all right for your blood relations?"

Yes, Eliza's Will remained as ever, still there remained annuities for them if they outlived her and there would also be an allowance towards her keep. After that she heard no more from her father.

When it was her Mother's birthday she sent her a portrait of herself, smiling, aged ten, and a love letter wishing her many happy returns. She heard nothing from her mother. She made one more attempt on her father's birthday but again heard nothing in reply.

Finally she filled a large cardboard box with things she could spare, to send to her family. There was a scarlet silk poplin frock for Betty Street, Margaret's daughter, amongst other things. She sent the whole lot to her sister Beatrice with plenty of stamps for her to forward to the people concerned. She asked her to give a big kiss to little Camille, her god child and daughter of her brother George. She had not been at the child's christening but had sent her a handsome silver and gilt porringer and spoon. How she wished she could visit these children, these little girls growing up into young women.

In reply she received letters from Beatrice and Betty, which she considered to be so callous that she tore them up, and wept. She reflected upon this strange family of hers. Mother, father, brothers and sisters, each going his own way, caring nothing for the others. At least when Margaret had sent her to the asylum it had been news enough for mother to write to Eddie in New Zealand to tell him. He read the letter and screamed out in anguish. The words leapt out at him from the page - his mother was promising to write to him again "If the worst comes to the worst and the Royal College of Surgeons get MacLoghlin's money"

Eddie wanted to swear, in the letter he wrote to Eliza, but would not.

Eliza had given them so much, presents and money, they all had cause to be grateful to her but she had not given them what they wanted, her obedience.

It was June before she was allowed to be accompanied by a keeper to Holland House to pack her clothes. There she was able to speak briefly to the women she had known for only a short time but whom she regarded as her friends. She collected her mail. Among the letters was one from the front, which read

'Percy Smith was killed on April 3rd 1916' Eliza wept for the poor sad boy who had had no one and had been so afraid of death. She wondered how badly he had suffered in the fields of Flanders.

Now she was to be admitted to a different asylum, St Ann's Heath in Virginia Water. This place seemed at first to be a much better, more caring, place where people might understand the mistake that had been made in treating her thus. But she was wrong. Nowhere was any different. Once the authorities had you in their clutches it was impossible to break free.

She wrote letters, her only means of contacting the outside world but they were never answered. Indeed she never knew whether they had been delivered, such was the censorship within this place. She would pour out her soul in her letters and sometimes she knew that to anyone reading them it would just seem to be so much drivel. 'Drivel', that was her word for most of what she wrote but she wrote it all the same, to anyone whom she thought might be able to help. Her Trustee, the Public Trustee was the man in whom she invested most of her trust. She wrote to him time and time again, pleading, flattering, cajoling - ail in the vain hope that he might take pity on her and come to her aid.

Only those who have known what it is like to be incarcerated in a place such as that can begin to appreciate what Eliza must have suffered in those long months, which stretched endlessly into each other.

As 1916 turned into 1917 and she was still there, in that dreadful place, she received news that the little Mim's mother, the beautiful actress had died in Holland House. She was only thirty-four years of age, had

had nothing in her life but sadness and loneliness and now her little boy was to know the same.

It was almost a year before she received any visitors, and then on one bitterly cold January day a handsome young airman called to see her. It was her husband's nephew, Jack MacLoghlin. How delighted she was to see him, to talk about his life and the war and to know that here was someone who did not think she was insane. He gave her sad news, however. His father, the doctor's brother, John had died the previous December. She felt now that she had no one in the world. He promised to write to her whenever he could but after that there was nothing. She was certain that he had been killed, and that no one had bothered to inform her.

Eliza tried to settle into the routine of life at St Ann's Heath. There were some in there who needed her attention and her love and she was only too happy to offer it. As she helped one old lady into dinner, the aged, neurotic woman let out a piercing scream and accused Eliza of squeezing her hand. Eliza protested, "I did not, I just pressed it affectionately" But that was not tolerated. She was ordered at once into the dread Gallery Number 3, a loathsome place, reserved for those who had committed some misdemeanor for which no other punishment could be found. Eliza did not protest further, she had learned that it served no purpose.

When the Official Solicitor called to see her some months later, he was unable to help. She pleaded with him to help her out of this place, to try to find a position for her, perhaps in a private house somewhere, with a family. He said he would do what he could, but after that she heard no more from him. She received no visitors, no letters, no news of her family, and all she could cherish was the memory of her beloved husband.

One evening in June she sat with some other inmates and began to sing to them. One or two of them started to laugh and the noise they made would not be tolerated by the authorities. Once more Eliza found herself in Gallery number 3, this time she was told it was because she was 'too tender and too exalted.'

Matron tried to intervene on her behalf but Eliza refused to be placated. She went on singing and she suffered the consequences. Her deafness was now acute. She was not always aware of how much noise she was making. She sang because she liked to make music and she no longer had a piano to play. Now she was not even allowed to sing.

After another year she received news which devastated her. The Public Trustee himself, sick in mind and body had been admitted to this same asylum. What hope was there for Eliza when the very man she had trusted to save her could not save himself?

As she went about her mundane tasks in the hospital she saw him, shuffling along accompanied by his attendant, hardly recognisable, so changed and sad was he. Eliza dropped her eyes and bowed briefly to the attendant. She heard later that it had been broken to him that he would never be able to return to his position as Public Trustee. How many times over the past three years had she wished he was her husband? She had sensed that he was attracted to her and why should he not be? she was still a beautiful woman. She was sure she could have helped him over his illness without it having to come to this. She remembered the time when her husband had been so very ill, three years before his eventual death, when she had been advised to send him to a Nursing Home, or did they mean Asylum?, before the strain of the whole situation drove them both out of their minds. But she refused; she would have refused to send her Trustee there as well.

There were signs now that the war was nearing its end and Eliza hoped that her personal war with bureaucracy and bigotry would soon end also.

She sat down now to write to her new Trustee. She was becoming desperate for companionship and her weary mind rambled as she wrote her letters. She had been happy during the short time at Holland House, looking after the women and their children. Now she wrote to Mr. Fulton, suggesting that he might find her a position with some gentleman or gentlewoman, someone who was independent but had no one to care for them. Mac had told her often how great she was in emergencies, how capable always and how sure he was that she was going to become even greater in time.

She read her letter over and realised with sadness that the strain of hoping, believing in others had worn her down. Any delusions she might have had were gone, she just lived now in the hope that some hand would reach out and pull her out of this pit, that she might leave everything behind, the wrongs she had suffered, the libel action. The world itself would be a better place when she was out of it.

The only people she could trust were the Trustee, the Official Solicitor and her brother Eddie at the other side of the world in New Zealand. Even he had made several journeys to England with his family, in fact it seemed that just as they had settled down in one country they moved back to the other, but he had paid no visits to her. She had now heard nothing from him for some time, but she knew that the war had made it difficult to send letters and parcels abroad, however she felt such an affinity with him that she knew the bond of love was stronger than any miles could sever.

She wrote once more to the Official Solicitor, enclosing a copy of the one to Leonard Fulton, and pleading that the two men should meet and discuss her case and then one of them should come to tell her what they had decided. She was only too aware of the problems involved in receiving visitors and she warned him to ask to see her privately, albeit for just a few minutes.

Eliza was still full of spirit and the will to fight. They could not crush that out of her. She had looked around her here in the asylum and it had become apparent that whatever she had understood to be Lunacy just did not exist. The so-called Lunatics who had been responsible for the devastation of the Great War had known what they were doing. Why else would they hit the Cathedral and spare the Asylum. No, the inmates of this institution were not Lunatics, some of them were very clever but difficult young people whose parents simply could not be bothered with them, and there were parents whose children could not be bothered with them. There were wives whose husbands had grown heartily weary of them and husbands whose wives were weary of them. There were a few who sat meditating on where they had gone wrong, still hoping, believing and groping for a way out. Together they and Eliza sat, healthy but growing old, the occasional functional derangement sliding into organic disease, there in their padded vaults.

For days Eliza wrote letters, outlining the treatment she was receiving and pleading to be helped out of this dreadful place. Always she kept copies of the letters she wrote because she never knew whether they had been received.

She was delighted to hear from Eddie once more, giving news of his children. She had written, begging him to call his next child Leonard after her trustee. Now she discovered that a daughter had been born and they had named her Leone. Eliza felt sure that this was in honour of her Trustee and she was overwhelmed with gratitude that Eddie and his wife had paid her such a tribute.

That week, on one of her rare visits into the town, she looked into a pawnshop window and saw a silver brooch, made in the form of a ram's head. She thought she had never seen anything so beautiful in her life. How she wanted to buy this and send it to Eddie, it was right that she should do this for he was after all living in a country renowned for its sheep and had even been called the Good Shepherd by his Maori friends.

However, the brooch cost five shillings and she had only one shilling in her purse. Entering the shop she pleaded with the Pawnbroker to reserve it for her for the one shilling deposit she had with her. He agreed and it seemed a long week before she was able to return with sufficient money to pay for it. Wrapping it carefully in a tiny silk bag she had received from another inmate of the asylum, she sent it to Eddie for his little daughter Nellie.

Her letters to her Trustee went unanswered. She pleaded that he would visit her, would set her free and tell her to go to New Zealand to her brother.

One of her treasured possessions was a first edition of a biography of Kate Greenaway written and presented to her by her dear friend Marian Spielmann. Now she took that and using the inside fly sheet of the book to write a letter, she parceled it up and received permission to send that to New Zealand also. When her brother received it his wife wondered why Eliza had so defaced the book by writing a letter on its pages, but they could have no Idea of the desperate measures Eliza would take to be able to contact people in freedom.

Now Eliza's thoughts were full of her brother and his family, both in her waking and sleeping moments. She was beset by nightmares and each day she would try to disentangle the confusing thoughts, with which she was left. Once she dreamed that Eddie had drowned and his widowed wife paced the sands with her children hoping for him to rise from the sea. She saw little Nellie wearing the ruby chameleon necklace she had sent her on her birth and she saw the child plunge into the sea and come out dragging a heavy burden. It was Eddie. He awoke on his back on the sand. When Eliza awoke she immediately sat down to write to Eddie, warning him to avoid swimming in the sea.

Collecting together all the copies of the letters she had sent to the various official bodies, she sent them to New Zealand to be read and then burned

.

Eddie read the letters; tears of compassion and anger welling in his eyes when he read of the treatment his sister had received. This painted a very different picture from the one his brother George had given him on his last visit to England. Then he had been led to believe that Eliza was mad, insane, and dangerous even and though he had hardly believed it he had chosen to do so. Now he felt a burden of guilt as he remembered that he had never visited her and had never given her a chance to explain things to him. It was unlikely that he would return to England again, the studio was thriving and his children were growing up. Now it seemed that New Zealand was to be their home forever.

It took him several hours to read through the pile of letters Eliza had sent him. He learned that Maggie had sent her to the Lunatic Asylum for what it was going to profit her.

One hundred and fifty pounds a year Eliza had left her as well as most of her personal belongings and her furniture and another hundred pounds to cover the cost of removals. It was not enough for Maggie; she wanted it then and more besides. She had determined that Eliza would change her mind about leaving money to the Royal College of Surgeons or she would die in the Asylum. But Eliza had survived, she had survived the beatings and she had never altered her Will, everything remained the same. Eliza hoped that in taking no revenge, this would heap coals of fire on the heads of those who had put her in this place.

Eddie determined to keep in touch with Eliza more regularly in the future, so that she would not feel quite so deserted by her family. He knew that neither her mother, father, brothers nor sisters ever visited her and only wrote occasionally. He himself was cut off from his family by distance. He wished she could join him out there and recover her health and strength in the warmth of New Zealand. As he stood looking out to sea, watching the waves breaking on the sandy beach, he felt free and happy but his heart ached for his sister.

When Eliza received the next letter from Eddie it was to tell her that he had indeed received the Kate Greenaway book, and the Ram's Head brooch. He enclosed photographs of his family and it delighted Eliza to see such a proud mother and father alongside their four happy, healthy children, John, Lillian, Nellie and Leone. How she wished to be able to visit them, play and laugh with them, teach them to play the piano, to sing and dance. In their stars she had seen that they would have talents such as those.

When, in November 1918, the war finally came to an end, her hopes were high for her own release. Why, she had read in 'The Times' that Sir Charles Stewart, the Public Trustee, whom she had seen in such despair in this asylum, was now fully restored to health. He was recuperating by the sea in Devonshire, and Eliza felt sure that contrary to general opinion, he would soon be reinstated in his official capacity.

She read in that same paper that Sir Alfred Gilbert, Sculptor, was living in Brighton, contented. A shiver ran down her spine as she thought of how cruelly that man had treated her. In fact she seemed to have been most cruelly treated by those she had loved and trusted.

She wrote to her brother in desperation. Surely he could find a good man who would be prepared to set Eliza free from this pit, marry her and take her out to New Zealand. She would not care whether the Royal College of Surgeons got a penny or not, she would alter her will in his favour and devote her life to his happiness. She knew she was still a beautiful woman. Although she was 55 years old she looked no more than 40, but in her heart she was a very old lady.

CHAPTER 11

The years dragged by and Eliza became somewhat reconciled to her life as a captive. She received occasional letters from her brother Eddie and from her father. However, they were always in the same vein, all she had to do, she realised, to gain her freedom, was to renounce her bequest to the Royal College of Surgeons and make a new Will in favour of her family. There were times when she was sorely tempted to give in to their blackmailing but she remained resolute. The bequest to the Royal College of Surgeons had been made out of love, the love she bore for her husband. The only reason she could possibly have for changing it was if she could feel that love for someone else. She wished she could find love like that once more. She certainly did not hold it for her family.

Eventually it was decided that an attempt should be made to rehabilitate Eliza. She was considered harmless enough by the authorities. Her moods which alternated between elation and depression were far more controlled. She was seen rather more as an object of pity and amusement than a danger to others.

Through her Solicitor and Trustee, Eliza had purchased a house in Marlborough Hill and it was there that she hoped to live out her days, with a maid for companionship. Her father was summoned and spent a long time discussing the situation with her Trustee. Her father agreed that she should come home with him and live in his house. He would be her guardian, would report on her progress and be responsible for her well-being. Matron, who understood only too well that it would not be well received, gave Eliza this news.

Eliza's heart sank. What choice did she have, go back to the shackles of her father or stay here in this place. She decided to comply with her father's wishes.

The train journey back to Wigan seemed endless. She barely spoke to her father nor he to her. Occasionally he would attempt some sort of conversation but was answered curtly. Eliza could only think that this pit to which she was now being taken might prove worse than the one she had just left.

Eliza was glad to see her mother again; it had been many, many years since they had last met. Susannah had grown old and tired, she felt she had little left to live for and even this reconciliation with her daughter was tinged with sadness because they both knew that Father was now in control as he had always intended to be.

That night Eliza found it strange to sleep in a warm comfortable bed and to find clean sheets upon it for the first time in years. She had brought only a few clothes with her since she had not had need for many in the asylum. The next day she intended to go out and buy herself some respectable clothes to wear.

However, money was now a large stumbling block. She had to ask for every penny and this was granted grudgingly at each request. Her Trustee had entrusted her father with twenty-five pounds of her money and he was going to eke this out for as long as possible. He had no intention of allowing Eliza to squander any of the money, which might eventually come to the family.

Eliza for her part was not going to give her father an easy task in looking after her. Whenever he allowed her to leave the house to walk in the park across the road from the house, she was watched from the window. She felt the eyes upon her and amused herself by trying to escape this gaze by hiding round corners and under bushes. The neighbours soon learned of this eccentric woman who was living with Mr. and Mrs. Millard. They heard it was their daughter and that she was insane. She saw mothers take hold of their children and drag them to safety as she passed by. How she longed to run and play with them, hold their hands and show them they had nothing to fear.

Eliza's love of children meant that she took delight in making friends with her nephews and nieces, some of whom she had never seen. She loved to visit her brother Billy and his lovely wife Jane and their children. Just as she had done years ago with her own younger sisters, she always took gifts for the girls, Doris, Aileen and baby Jean, particularly Aileen in whom she saw the beautiful young woman she once was herself. But for little Billy there was nothing. Never again would she give presents to a boy or a man. She had broken this rule only once since she was so deeply hurt by Alfred Gilbert, that was when she foolishly, or so she felt, bought a birthday present for Maggie's son, Alex, and she had been rewarded by being carted off to an Asylum. No, boys could look after themselves. She took a certain delight in putting them in their place. On one occasion she had taken the family a treat for their meal, some shrimps. Young Billy, who already, at six years old was intelligent and highly perceptive, had never seen shrimps before but knew they lived in the sea. He took a bowl of water, added salt and placed the shrimps in it, hoping to see them swim. The poor dead creatures lay inert in the water and he looked on in dismay. He went to Eliza and asked why they would not swim.

She looked at him with the contempt she reserved for men in general and said disparagingly "Because they are dead, you silly little boy". Billy was to remember her look and her words for the rest of his life.

When Eliza's brother George came to visit, it was to try to talk Eliza into 'considering her parents' by being more generous to them in her Will. Margaret had certainly made sure that they were all well informed about the contents of this Will which was causing everyone such anguish.
George Invited Eliza to stay with him and his family for a few days, to give his parents a break from the responsibilities. George had married a French woman, Camille, a charming, gracious lady who reminded Eliza

very much of her own mother. They had five children, Suzanne (known as Fifi), Georges, Helene, Camille and Yvonne. Life in that household was strict but happy, George was a schoolmaster, loved and respected by his pupils. He demanded the same respect in his home. The children were all academically gifted and it was expected that they would go to Universities and into the professions.

Eliza stayed with them on a few occasions but was always glad to leave; she found life there almost as restrictive as the asylum. They spoke only French in the house and Eliza felt threatened by her inability to communicate.

It was not an easy time for any of them. The years spent in institutions had taken their toll on Eliza and she found it hard to adjust to the relative freedom. No one realised that she would need help and time in coming to terms with her new life. It was expected that she would just pick up where she had left off, almost ten years before. The fact that she did not adjust easily was taken as even more proof of her instability.

While she had been in the asylum, it had been made possible for her to visit the Royal College of Surgeons at fairly frequent intervals, to sit by Mors Janua Vitae and just feel herself to be near the casket containing her husband's ashes. One day she would join him there and this would be their home for eternity. Now, living two hundred miles away in Wigan she could not make the journey by herself and no one in the family was willing to accompany her. The very mention of 'Macloghlin' sent her father into a rage. Her brother George was almost as bad. There was no way her brother Billy could take her, having a business to run and a wife who was far from well. The only possibility was for her sister Beatrice to accompany her. Beatrice still lived at home with her parents and since Eliza's return they had been fairly good friends again.

It was agreed that Beatrice and Eliza would travel by train to London, at Eliza's expense and would spend a few days in Eliza's house at Marlborough Hill. This would give Beatrice the opportunity to see how well Eliza could cope if she were to remain there alone. Eliza was filled with delight at the prospect of returning to London and her lover. It meant that she would be free from the clutches of her father. Beatrice noted saw the change in Eliza and began to see her as quite a different person from the one always described by her father and George. Billy had always been prepared to live and let live, he had little time for gossip and Jack had just thought Eliza was a bit odd. George was the one who had made such a great issue of the whole affair.

Once in London, Eliza became almost her old self again, visiting friends and shopping for clothes. Just occasionally a cloud would descend over her and she would become cold and sad once more. Beatrice tried to discuss with Eliza the date of their return to Wigan but Eliza would not join in. Eliza had decided she was not returning to Wigan but she did not know how she was going to tell Beatrice, nor what would be her response.

Eventually, during the obligatory visit to her Trustee, Eliza broached the subject of remaining in London, in her own home, accompanied by a maid. Beatrice was horrified at the suggestion but the Trustee thought it an excellent idea. It was a difficult enough job for him to keep an eye on Eliza's affairs while she was in London. It had been virtually impossible while she was in Wigan. For his part it would be the best move.

With his support, Beatrice felt able to return home and break the news to her father and brothers. James Millard's reaction was not what Beatrice had expected. She had thought he would have been angry with her for allowing Eliza to remain in London. She thought he would be sorry to have lost Eliza again after having her at home for some time. However, he seemed resigned to the fact that she had pleased herself yet again. His main concern appeared to be that now he was not in a position to persuade her to change her Will.

Eliza's life now became happy and carefree. She answered to no one, apart from her weekly visits to her Trustee where she was always on her best behaviour. She visited the Royal College of Surgeons as often as possible and the staff there were amused by her presence. She would drift in and out as if she owned the place.

One day, as she was sorting through some old papers, she came across the carefully collected letters, which she had received from Alfred Gilbert. She read them through and wondered what she should do with them. This was an episode in her life which had caused her great distress. She had felt a kind of love for Gilbert, and she knew from these letters that he had felt the same for her. However, she no longer needed to keep them. She could not bring herself to destroy them and so she decided they should be returned. But where was he living? He was rarely mentioned in the newspapers these days and if she were to make any attempt to discover his whereabouts, this was sure to be misconstrued.

She knew what she must do. She wrote a letter to her dear friend Marian Spielmann. She knew his address and knew that he would help her. However she must be careful not to hurt the poor man. He was still, she was certain, madly in love with her himself and if he were to think that she was still thinking about Gilbert, then he would be mortally hurt. She rambled on in her letter to Spielmann about her life and the way she had been wronged and how she hoped he had forgiven her for deserting him and hoped he was well and that Gilbert was well.

She sent the letter and awaited the reply.

When Marian Spielmann received the letter he was totally at a loss as to how to reply. This was a strange letter indeed and one for which there appeared to be no purpose. He had heard nothing of this lady, for whom he had had the highest regard, for many years. He realised now why he had heard nothing, He put the letter to one side, intending to reply when he had decided what to say. When he came to reply to it, however, it was nowhere to be found. He could only assume that the maid had thrown it out with some other papers. Now, he had no address to which to reply and so he tried to put the matter out of his mind.

Eliza was becoming impatient for a reply from Spielmann. She felt deserted, scorned. Her anger began to grow at the way she was being treated, by men, again. One day she took all Gilbert's letters and parceled them together with a note reading, 'His property'.

She now wondered whether Spielmann had ever received her letter, perhaps he was no longer at that address. So she sent them to the Garrick Club of which he was a member and where he would be bound to get them. However, Spielmann was no longer a member there and the parcel was duly returned to her. Distraught, she refused to believe that they could not find him and she put the whole parcel in another cover and returned it to the Garrick Club. This time attempts were made to contact Spielmann and he received the package of letters. He wrote to Eliza explaining his reasons for not replying to her letter. His letter was kind and Eliza's heart warmed when she read that he had written to remind the author of a new book about Alfred Gilbert and his art that he must be sure to refer to Mors Janua Vitae in the book. He promised to forward the parcel to Gilbert.

What Gilbert did when he received the letters is not clear. It is certain that his family made sure they were never made public, as they did with the letters which she had written to him.

Another sad episode in Eliza's life was now over. She had little to do with her time now and whenever possible went where there were children to watch and to play with. The Zoo was just such a place. She loved to see the pleasure on the faces of the children but she also hated to see the way the animals were kept in captivity. She stood one day watching a rhinoceros pacing laboriously around its caged enclosure. She reached out to it in friendship.

"Come to me you poor creature," she pleaded.

The animal trundled towards her and saw the glistening of her ring. Opening its mouth it took Eliza's hand and sunk its teeth into the gold ring. Eliza screamed out in pain and the animal relaxed its grip. She painfully bound the bleeding and almost severed finger with her handkerchief and hid the hand inside her coat. People who had heard her screams came to her aid but she would show no one the wound and would accept no help. She was afraid of allowing herself to be at the mercy of anyone again.

Once home, almost fainting from the pain in her finger, she began her own treatment. Taking a jar of Marmite, she smeared it over the wound. She knew that this contained yeast, which would act as an antiseptic. Hourly she renewed the dressings but the wound remained as bad as ever. She then tried Honey, which she knew contained healing properties but neither of these gave her any relief from the pain. At last, in desperation, her bandaged arm in a sling, she went to the Royal College of Surgeons and pleaded that they amputate the finger. Used to this strange woman, the staff there tried to tell her that this was a College and not a hospital but she would hear none of this. Eventually, to placate her, an appointment was made for her to see one of the surgeons in his consulting rooms.

Almost demented with the pain she took a cab to her Trustee's Office. She pleaded with him to help her, to get her into a private hospital where she could be cared for and her finger healed.

She was admitted on April 20th 1928 to Ticehurst Hospital in Sussex. This was a beautiful Private Asylum, in acres of magnificent grounds, tended by gardeners. Wealthy families of the inmates drove up daily; there were servants, and greenhouses and the hospital had its own pack of harriers. As its social status grew, patients were drawn from all over Britain as well as from overseas. Here surely, Eliza could feel contented.

But although she had requested that she go to this place, once there she felt trapped. She was free to leave the hospital at will, only the most frail and confused patients being locked up. However, she knew that this was to be her lot for the rest of her days. By asking to be brought here, she had now admitted to herself and to the world at large that she was mad.

Her finger was now beginning to heal but she still experienced a great deal of pain. There were many people there, like herself, wealthy and lonely, victims of their families' greed and intolerance. They were classified by the degree or type of their madness. Some, such as Eliza, were classified as chronic maniacs, others paranoid, some manic-depressives. The factor common to them all was their loneliness and inability to communicate their feelings to the people who could help them. The beauty of their surroundings did not compensate for the freedom to love and be loved and for being part of a loving family. More beautiful than the other places this might be, she still saw the same signs, the dead eyes staring out from sunken cheeks. People dying from illnesses totally unrelated to their madness but untreated because of it. Men wandering the corridors crying for their mothers and found later, decapitated on the railway line. What did it matter that they were paying vast sums of money to live here, the result would be the same, and they would never go out alive. Occasionally some did leave to be transferred to other less costly places, probably when their families thought that too much of their own inheritance was being frittered away. Some more fortunate ones were taken to live out their lives in their own homes under supervision.

There was still the same smell in this place as there had been in all the others. It settled in Eliza's nose and throat and remained with her all the time.

Each day a dish was placed on the mantelpiece, containing Carbolic Acid. This was intended to disinfect the room. Eliza began to see this as her salvation, her way out when other plans had failed. She waited until the others had left the room and then carefully carried the boat-shaped dish to her own room.

No one noticed that Eliza had not appeared on the morning of the first of May. Those who chose to stay in bed were allowed to do so. Those who caused trouble were the ones who needed the help of the staff. It was late morning when a maid went to tidy Eliza's room and found her crouched by the side of the bed, holding her stomach, her face contorted with pain. The maid called for help and Eliza was lifted on to the bed. Blisters around her mouth gave them the first clue as to what she had done. The empty Carbolic Acid dish confirmed their suspicions. She had drunk the entire contents and must have spent the night in agony as the acid successively burned her mouth, throat, gullet and stomach. She died as they stood by the bed.

No Post mortem was ordered, as the cause of death was quite clear. An inquest held on the third of May returned a verdict of Suicide by poisoning, by taking Carbolic Acid whilst of unsound mind.

Her family had to be notified of Eliza's death and arrangements made for her cremation at Golders Green Crematorium. According to the instructions she had laid down so explicitly in her Will, her body was completely veiled with the white silk crepe veil kept In the casket she had prepared for her ashes. Her sister Beatrice travelled down to London for the funeral along with her brothers Jack and Alfred. It was a sombre affair with no religious ceremony and few people present. It hardly seemed worth the journey, they felt. In fact what they had really come for was to make things look right in view of their true reasons for making the journey. Immediately after the Cremation, the three of them went to the Public Trustee's Office to see how matters stood as regards her Will. They discovered that beyond the annuities to her parents and Maggie and the gifts to Maggie and Beatrice, the rest would go to the Royal College of Surgeons; Ten thousand pounds and the residue of her estate for the purpose of founding and endowing Scholarships for medical students in memory of her husband. Although they had always known that this was the case, somehow they had always lived in hopes. The Public Trustee could not give them much hope but suggested they approach the Royal College of Surgeons.

George and Jack were then deputed by the family to meet the President who received them and heard their suggestion that the College should take sufficient for the scholarship and leave the rest to be divided amongst the family. He appeared to take kindly to the idea but advised them to go away and instruct a lawyer to send an official letter embodying the proposals.

George was now taking charge of the situation. The letter was duly commissioned. However, they discovered that since the original Will had been written in 1910 and she had not been certified as insane until 1913, nothing could be done to alter the terms of the Will. If they were to fight the case it was doubtful whether what they received, if they won, would even cover their expenses.

Eliza's plans for the disposal of her ashes were again carried out to the letter. None of her family attended the short ceremony in the lobby of the Royal College of Surgeons. The Assistant Secretary of the College, Kennedy Cassels, along with Eliza's Solicitor, were there as the cinerary urn was opened and her ashes were mingled with those of her late husband. The casket was locked, for eternity, and the keys subsequently destroyed. They were re-united at last; their love had triumphed over the greed and hypocrisy of her family; they would remain there for ever, looking down upon visitors and students alike at the Royal College of Surgeons of England. Young men would benefit from the Macloghlin Scholarships and would follow in the footsteps of a great but little acknowledged doctor. It was doubtful whether any of them would ever know how the life of one lady had been sacrificed in her determination to make sure that those scholarships existed.

CONCLUSION

It was September, four months after Eliza's death, that George finally decided to write and inform Eddie in New Zealand.

The true facts were not given however, George preferring to say that she had died from gangrene as a result of the rhinoceros bite. The letter explained that they had not informed him and his brother Jim in America earlier because the family feared that they might come rushing over at their own expense thinking there would be something for them in the Will. There being nothing of course, it would all have been a waste of time and money. Everything, George insisted, had been done at the request of the family in England.

"Anyway" he wrote, "she has gone and there is nothing for us"

He then turned to the much more important details of his family's successes at school and University.

When Eddie received George's letter, he wept for his poor sad sister and was horrified at the treatment she was still receiving from her family even after her death. He tried to reply many times but could never find the right words.

"How can you scream in a letter?" he asked his wife.

Printed in Great Britain
by Amazon

87470157R00127